T0130492

A
Way
To A
Man's Heart
1

CREOLE COOKBOOK

by

SANDRA J. SYLVEST-GALLE-GOUDEAUX

To order additional copies of this book, contact:
Xlibris
844-714-8691
www.Xlibris.com
Orders@Xlibris.com

ISBN: Softcover   978-1-6641-5634-0
        Hardcover   978-1-6641-5635-7
        EBook   978-1-6641-5633-3

Library of Congress Control Number: 2021902377

Print information available on the last page

Rev. date: 02/12/2021

CONTENTS

IS IT TRUE WHAT THEY SAY ABOUT NEW ORLEANS' CREOLE WOMEN?!?

Is it true that grace and charm run through their veins? Is it true that Creole Women process a God-given talent and ability to set the tone for just about anything they are involved in and she can master them all? Is it true that the spirit of love and hospitality is personified in her?

Creole women of old were steeped in their culture and traditions which brought about generations of family values. These women passed down these values to their families. They were eager to teach and to guide not only their families but whoever they came in contact with within the community.

Serving God and a prayer life was a vital part of the creole family's life. Coming from a long line of praying women, I know this to be true. My grandmother, Eugenia Duplessis-Cornin, was a powerful praying woman of God. She not only prayed for her grandchildren but she would also bless us with holy water (remember, we were Catholics). Yes, she gave me hugs, kisses, fruit, and would bless me every time we met. You see that was the way of the creole family, greeting one another with a hug and a kiss.

From a little girl maybe three or four years old, I can still remember my grandmother would bless me every time I visited her. She called me "Mag's Baby". I never could understand it because I was the second to the oldest of four children. As a child, I would chuckle about it, I dared not let anyone see me. I thought it was cute.

The Creoles of New Orleans were devoted Catholics in those days. Oh yes, especially in the Sixth Ward where I grew up. The families there promoted family living and family support. We had nurturing fathers and nurturing mothers, coupled in togetherness not just for their family but for everyone in the neighborhood. We truly had a village. This kind of caring and nurturing grew strong back in the days in New Orleans and the surrounding areas of Southern Louisiana. Parents taught their children to show love and respect not only to their family members but also to their fellow man. However, what you did with it once you left the nest was totally up to you. Some of us held on to our family values and traditions but sadly to say some did their own thing. But let it not be said we were not taught, or guided in the right way, or not given a foundation of who God is and how important it is to serve Him and to have Him in our lives. Instilling the love of God in the family was a key factor in Creole's everyday life. My mama uses to say, "treat people the way you want them to treat you" and she would say, "people will be people, but God says to love, so you love them and treat them with a long-handled spoon". Mama would also say, "my child, you can't make it in this world by yourself, you need Jesus". To this day, I still hold and cherish the many, many words my mother would say to me. Some of these words made me become the person I am today. I love because it is commanded by God.

Most of us grew up in bilingual and multilingual homes (Creole, English, French, & Italian) which was the norm for New Orleans sixth, seventh wards, and the surrounding parishes of Louisiana. We have a rich heritage of Creole culture and Creole cuisine. Oh yes, this is my reason for putting this book together. My book has been a long time coming, but I could not take it to the grave with me. No, not all of our everyday meals, Thanksgiving, Christmas, and all other holidays, that were celebrated in pure creole style so rich in love and flavor. I say Yummy to the gumbos, the stuffed, the unstuffed, the beans, the baked, the unbaked, the jambalaya, the cakes, and the pies. I will continue to eat up and I will continue to keep it moving creole style.

x | SANDRA J. SYLVEST-GALLE-GOUDEAUX

DEDICATION

To My Mother
Mrs. Marguerite Marie Cornin-Sylvest
July 20, 1922 - March 28, 1975

My mother's heart was always filled with love and it showed in everything she did, family, friends, neighbors, and even strangers who would show up at our front door from time to time. There was always a feeling of peace and security in our home. My mother's words were always soothing to the spirit and soul, encouraging to the heart, and wise yet gentle to the ears. Her words were seasoned with wisdom and love, for God had given her a nurturing spirit. She welcomed her family and friends with open arms and always would have time to listen, to pray, and to help ease their pain.

I can truly say Mama, Marg, Auntie Mag, MaGlett (her creole nickname), was a strong pillar in her family. I am saying all this to say, mama loved people and she loved to cook, to share a meal with whoever, and to do whatever she could for them. She fed everyone and I do mean everyone that came through our doors and you could actually feel and taste the love in every one of her dishes. Mama had a spirit of hospitality in her heart, her spirit, and her soul. That was my mama!

I never understand how, no matter how many people came through our doors, mama had enough for all. This puzzled me so that every once and a while, I would walk over to the stove, uncover the pot, and look in just knowing I would see the pot going deep into the stove, needless to say, it never happened. All I saw was mama's same pot sitting on the same burners, sitting on the same old stove. I began to realize that it was God who gave her the increase so I named my mother's pots, "Mama's Bottomless Pots" for God always gave her more than enough.

I remember as a child how I would wait very patiently for my mama's homemade cakes and pies to come out of the oven. The smell of vanilla and butter would fill the air. Some of you remember your grandmother and your mother homemade cakes, in went the straw (you remember the broom straw, all grandmothers used them). Later it went from a broom straw to a toothpick. Straw/toothpick into the cake, out clean, the cake is done. Those were the days, the beautiful days of way back when. Sixth Ward, Gov. Nicholls Street, Sylvest home days. From mama's butter pound cakes to her buttery sweet potato pies, to her file' or okra gumbo, to her stuffed mirliton, it was all delicious and all were seasoned in love.

Thank you, my mother, for being the mama I needed in my life and your effectual fervent prayers thus making me who and what I am today. And thanks to the people who bought my book. May it bring joy and happiness to everyone who partakes of its recipes and may your food always be seasoned with love like my mama's from God up above.

ACKNOWLEDGEMENTS

MY FATHER
Charley J. Sylvest
October 21, 1922 - June 4, 1991

When I was a child and needed a father, my dad was always there for me. Not only was he a good father but he was a good husband, son, brother, uncle, neighbor, and friend. Daddy, you taught me how to stand up for myself, how to speak up for myself, how to make decisions, and how to stand on the decisions I made. You made me strong and I thank you for it.

Daddy, you helped me in my relationship with God, my heavenly father, in so many ways. For you were a father that knew how to give good earthly gifts to your children, just as God gave good heavenly gifts to His children. God blessed me with a father I could trust, one I could look up to, and one that I could respect. Thus enabling me to easily trust in my Heavenly Father and to form the relationship I need to have with Him to make it in this world.

My father had the spirit of excellence. He was a chief not only was his food delicious but his food presentation was superb. I had the best of both worlds mama's creole cooking and daddy's traditional cooking. I love you "Da" for that is what I called you and thank you for being my daddy.

And I say this with much love and respect. Daddy, I never would have made it without YOU in my life! You gave me your best.

MY BROTHER
Charles J. Sylvest
September 30, 1948 - August 30, 1988

As children, we stood back to back in every situation. Our childhood days were full of fun and laughter. He was a thoughtful and caring brother, and you were my friend. Charlie had a good heart but I must say he did not take any mess. He called a spade a spade and that was one of the many things I loved about him. I miss you my brother and this is another reason, that I press toward the mark of the high calling of God, knowing I will see you again. Thank you, my dear brother, for loving me and looking out for me in life, I love you. And with this, I say from the depths of my heart. Brother, I never would have made it without you on my side!

MY LOVING AUNT
Alice Cornin-Encalade

She was my mother's closest sister, my favorite aunt, and she was like a grandmother to me. She was a force to be reckoned with, she spoke her mind in a loving way and our family loved her for what she stood for truth and strength.

Thank you, Auntie Alice, for being there for me and not only for me but for my whole family. Thank you for the love and kindness you showed to me as a child. You always made me feel special. You called me, "My Samp". And your Samp says to you this day thank you. Auntie, I will always love, love, love you. I would have never made it without you in my life!

MY AUNT
Esther Corinin-Gaunichaux-LaPage

My mother and my Auntie were sisters and they were very close. Auntie Bay (her Creole nickname) would visit her every day. They loved each other so much and it showed in everything they did for each other. Auntie Bay, thank you for being a loving aunt. She uses to call me "Sa San". One of her sons calls me "Sampa" until this very day. That was the nickname he gave to me. Hi Cuz, Charles J. Gaunichaux, love you. Love you auntie and I thank you for being in my life when I needed an Aunt.

MY BIRTH MOTHER
Syrilla M. Kennedy-Glapion

I call her my birth mother because she helped bring me into this world. She was our next-door neighbor. I will always have a special place in my heart for her. Her oldest daughter is my godmother. I love you. The Sylvest and Glapions were like family.

Mrs. Glap, I want to thank you for being there for my mother on that bright September morning. It was a Sunday morning. You were there to assist my mother in welcoming me into the world. To a sweet, kind, loving, and praying woman who loved me and watched over me when I was a child, I say thank you. Ms. Glap for this is what I called her, I never would have made it without you on that beautiful Sunday morning!

SPECIAL THANKS

Bertha Smith-Johnson
One of my oldest and dearest friends. (52 years of friendship)

I call her, "The River", for she is an ever-flowing vessel of love and compassion for family and friends. There is not enough paper and time for me to express our friendship and our walk together with our mothers, fathers, sisters, and brothers. May God continue to bless you for you being a blessing to many and to me. Be strong my friend, know that God loves you and I do too.

Patrica A. Johnson-Smith
My very first friend in California. (34 years of friendship)

I call her, "The Visionary and The Encourager".

You always have been a blessing and a faithful friend. You are a Stirrer Upper for God uses her to always remind me of His call, His plan, and His purpose for my life. And needless to say, you are always on point and on time. Pat, I want to thank you for playing such a vital part in my life though-out the years. For you are that earthly friend that sticks closer than any brother or sister. Love you, my dear friend and sister in Christ.

Mary Jane Lunia-Davis
My God-given sister. (34 years of friendship)

I call her "The Rock" for her faithfulness in standing on the word of God.

M J, you are a force to be reckoned with. You are not only a true friend but God gave you to me as a blood sister because He knew what I needed. You are the sister that loves, prays, and believes the Word of God for me. May you be blessed exceedingly in all you think, say, or do. May God's light shine upon you in your going out and in your coming in.

Love you, my dear sister and friend. I am so glad God gave us to each other as sisters. God calls you faithful and God calls you friend.

I Appreciate all of your praying, believing, trusting, and the support you guys have shown to me through the years, thank you. Love you and may God continue to bless and to keep you.

INTRODUCTION

This is a picture of me at the age of four. I attended Martinez Nursery and this is my yearbook picture.

I chose this photo because this is where my journey began. The happy times, the good food, and the many things it took to make a child's life wonderful. This book is based on my life as a child growing up in New Orleans, Sixth Ward. My elementary school days attending Saint Peter Claver. It tells of the dishes the people prepared and enjoyed on a daily basis. Growing up in my sixth ward neighborhood, I was always surrounded by a good family, food, neighbors, and friends. The Creole way of doing things was respect, love, and happiness. In New Orleans back in the day's grandfathers, grandmothers, fathers, mothers, aunts, and uncles made it all work. There was much respect for your fellow man, adults were adults, and children were allowed to be children. Playing jacks, shooting marbles, jumping rope, riding bicycles, roller skating, were some of the things we did as kids. We had fun, fun, fun.

In our community, everyone went to church on Sunday. My family went to mass and after mass, it was donut time. Yes, we ate donuts for breakfast every Sunday after church.

My favorite was powdered jellies, I had two jellies with a tall glass of milk. Mass was early in the morning so mama would order them with your choice of milk. This would hold us over until dinner which was usually about two o'clock. Great family dinners on Sunday were of the norm. Invitations flowed to come and dine but invitation or not family and friends were always welcome. No one was turned away for hospitality flowed through the street in our communities. All you can eat and take some home for your mama and tell her we said hello.

Mondays were always red bean day. A lot of the restaurants in New Orleans still honor Monday as Red Bean Day with all kinds of luncheon specials. Back in the day, it was Red Beans with your choice of meat. Fried chicken, pork chop, fish, hot sausage, and smoked sausage were some of the favorites. My choice would always be fried chicken or hot sausage.

In my seventh and eighth grades at Saint Peter Claver, my parents would let me go to lunch with some of my classmates and friends on some Saturdays. Our favorite place to go was Dookie Chase Restaurant on Orleans Avenue. With all of the delicious Creole cuisine serve there, I would always order a Hot Sausage on French "Po-Boy" dressed with extra pickles and mayonnaise and a cold glass of root beer soda. In New Orleans, sodas were called soft drinks. There were several moms and pops sweet shops with all sorts of goodies Po-Boy sandwiches, fried chicken, and fish plates with New Orleans style potato salad as one of the sides. I can't leave out the sweets of my childhood days pralines, fudge, popcorn balls, hand suckers, soft drinks, frozen cups, and snowballs are just to name a few. All were homemade lip-smacking, and finger-licking good. Almost every sweet shop had a specialty of its own and the kids of our neighborhood would walk, run, skate, ride our bikes making our way to each and every one of them.

I not only did the recipes but I added little captions about them. The way it was with me and my childhood living in the sixth ward of New Orleans. All of the delicious foods, the music, and the creole culture which flow to all parts of the city made us truly blessed.

I am taking this time to thank you for purchasing a copy of my book. May you enjoy each and every one of its recipes. May all of your family and friends' gatherings be filled with joy and happiness. And may the people feel and taste your love in each and every bite.

NEW ORLEANS BEVERAGES

Some of the drinks and remedies of the way it was Sixth Ward Styles New Orleans. And all of them are still used, drank and enjoyed today

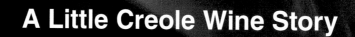

A Little Creole Wine Story

Saluting the Strong Creole Heritage of winemaking. All the grandmas and the great-grandmas made their wine and shared it with their families and friends. Back in the days of old. New Orleans and the surrounding areas. We had a village. And hats off to today's generations who are keeping it alive.

NEW ORLEANS BEVERAGES

Some of the drinks and remedies of the way it was Sixth Ward Styles New Orleans. And all of them are still used, drank and enjoyed today

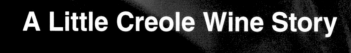

A Little Creole Wine Story

Saluting the Strong Creole Heritage of wimemaking. All the grandmas and the great-grandmas made their wine and shared it with their families and friends. Back in the days of old. New Orleans and the surrounding areas. We had a village. And hats off to today's generations who are keeping it alive.

STORYTIME "CREOLE HOMEMADE WINE"

Hold it! I can not go a step further without spreading the word about Creole homemade wines. I want to talk about the wines that were made in our family. Oh, oh Auntie Alice I am about to tell on you. Creole people of New Orleans and the surrounding areas were noted for making their brews. My auntie Alice was the supplier to my immediate family, lol and she was so cute about it.

She lived in Plaquemine Parish, Louisiana about thirty miles south of New Orleans. It always made a great trip when we would visit her after mass on some Sundays. Down the river road, we'd go with roast, potato salad, cake, pie, etc you name it. Creoles never go anywhere empty-handed. Needless to say, Auntie Alice somehow would always know we were coming. She would have all kinds of goodies ready for us gumbo, quail, wild duck, rabbit stew, etc. We had other family members who lived in the area (Auntie Pill and Uncle Hunter to name a few) and it would be creole dining at its best.

Everything always started at Aunt Alice's house. We would turn left off of the river road into the property lane, jump out of the car, grab the goodies from the trunk, and trail blaze about a block down the lane to her house and get ready for the fun. A whole lot of hugs & kisses, food, and laughter. My Auntie Alice was one of the most loved people in our family.

I remember as a child the adults were always served a glass of wine with their gumbo. But as a child, our glass had only about a once of wine in it. I remember she would say, "it is as clear as a bell", whatever that meant. My auntie would say, "My Samp, let auntie show you something". We would go into the living room, she would point to the sofa. I would notice her sofa would always be pulled away from the wall. She would point to the sofa and say to me, "go see". Low and behold behind the sofa were rows of gallons of wine. And behind her bed in her bedroom, she kept it cater-cornered were crockpots. Two will be ready for Thanksgiving and two will be ready for Christmas. My eyes would stretch and she would just laugh. Winemaking is the norm in the Creole families of southern Louisiana. There was at least one winemaker in every family. Blackberry, Elderberry, Grape, Strawberry, Peach Brandy just to name a few.

I thank God for the good times that were spent with Aunts and uncles, sisters and brothers, cousins, and friends living and loving in the communities of Southern Louisiana during the Fifties and the early Sixties back in the days.

HOLIDAY EGGNOG

Homemade Egg Nog was a must at every holiday celebration. From Thanksgiving to New Year's Eve, it graced every punch bowl and every large pot of almost every home in the Sixth & Seventh Wards. Creole egg nog was never made with vanilla. It was added to your cup or glass for those who did not drink alcohol but still wanted the taste of whiskey in their cup. You would hear the people say, "bring out the whiskey & bring in the eggnog". It wasn't until later people began using brandy and rum in their drink. Two things I do know for sure about eggnog is that it is rich, and it is true New Orleans. Served hot or cold it is one of New Orleans ' most favorite drinks.

If you want a richer tasting nog add more eggs, less rich fewer eggs.

Drink up and be happy!

7 cups milk (whole)

1 cup cream (evaporated)

1 cup sugar (to taste)

6 egg yolks

1 tbsp nutmeg (to taste)

1/8 tsp salt (to taste)

2 tsp pure vanilla extract (optional)

2 tbsp whiskey (optional)

Pour milk into a large pot. Heat over medium setting. Slowly bring milk to all most a boil. Turn off heat right before boiling. Separate egg yolks from the eggs. Beat egg yolks together until fluffy. Combine sugar, nutmeg & salt. Add slowly into yolks and mix slowly. Mix 2 cups of hot milk from the pot slowly into eggs. Mix slowly (2 minutes). Next, pour the mixture into your pot. Cook over low-med heat. Do not allow it to come to a boil. Next, add cream to the pot. Stirring constantly (5-7 minutes) or until thickened. Add whiskey and/or vanilla (optional). Let cool before refrigerating. Can be served hot or cool. Enjoy.

Yield: 1 gallon

MAMA YA YA

Mama Ya-Ya is one of the oldest grandma's remedies for the New Orleans party time hangovers. Sample but it will do the trick. Ask the creole senior citizens about it. I know they will have some tall stories to tell. Including some of my big cousins means older cousin in New Orleans). I am not saying any names but you know who you are. I would hear the doorbell early in the morning. I would hear mama say to my cousin, "child where have you been and where do you think you're going?". Auntie Mag I... Mama would say "I don't want to hear it". She would go to the kitchen, warm up the milk for their tonic. I dare you to come to my house drunk. Now I have to get you straight. What is my sister going to say about this"? Mama Ya-Ya has saved a lot of souls. And that the way it was in the neighborhoods.

4 ozs milk

1-2 jiggers whiskey (100% proof)

1 tsp honey (to taste)

1/4 tsp cinnamon stick

2 fresh mint leaves

cinnamon (sprinkle top)

1 Place milk and whiskey in a saucepan.

2 Bring almost to a boil.

3 Pour into a large mug.

4 Add honey and stir.

5 Sprinkle cinnamon on top.

6 Add cinnamon stick.

7 Garnish with mint leaves.

8 Relax and enjoy.

MAMA'S MINT TEA *

This was one of my mother's favorite teas. I remember as a little girl mama had a little mint bush in the backyard. She would say mint tea was for special guests. But every Sunday no matter who came to dinner, she would scurry down the back steps straight to her little mint bush. She would carefully pick leaves from it. My brother, Charlie would lean over and say to me, "I guess everybody is special". I would just laugh and say, "yes everyone is special to mama". She brewed her tea sometimes just using the mint, sometimes with lemons, with fruit, and sometimes she would add tea bags. Everyone loved her teas. It was so refreshing.

8 cups water

Honey/Sugar (to taste)

5-6 mint leaves

3-4 lemons (sliced)

1/2 vanilla (pure)

Bring 4 cups water to a boil in a saucepan. Remove from heat. Add mint leaves & cover. Let steep for 10-20 minutes. Strain tea. Add honey/sugar stirring until dissolved. Add vanilla, three squeezed lemons, and four cups of cold water. Refrigerate until ready to serve. Fill glasses with ice. Can add grapes or sliced strawberries to glass. Garnish with lemon and mint. Or you can serve this tea hot.

Yield:3 quarts

FRIDAY NIGHT HOT COCO

Yield: 6 cup

TGIF is not just for today. I would say yay it's Friday. One day vacation on Saturday from mass, school, uniforms, and homework during the week. Now it was time for hot cocoa and my mama's homemade buttery biscuits. She would cut them in different shapes and sizes. My favorite was her drop biscuits, they were to die for. We could stay up late, watch the tv until it goes off. Sometimes mama would make a sweet buttery cornbread to go with our hot chocolate. I still to this day make biscuits to go along with my hot chocolate. It always brings back the sweet little memories of the way it was and what we did. Those little things so sweet and never forgotten.

5 cups milk

1/3 cup cocoa powder (unsweeten)

3/4 sugar (to taste)

1/2 cup cream

1/2 cup water

1 tsp pure vanilla

salt (pinch)

1 Combine cocoa, sugar, and salt in saucepan.

2 Add water. to pan.

3 Heat on low medium.

4 Bring mix to boil (2 to 3 minutes).

5 Stir to keep from scorching.

6 Next pour in milk and let heat until very hot.

7 Do not let cocoa come to a boil.

8 Remove from heat.

9 Stir in cream and vanilla.

10 May add whip topping or marshmallows.

11 You are all set to go.

MAMA'S HOT TADDY

Yield: 1 serving

Generation after generation has used this tonic for added relief from colds and the flu. My grandmother used it. Her children used it. And needless to say, I share it with everyone I could. The skeptics said it would not work, folklore. I say try it for yourself, the proof is in the pudding. Down south in the land of the creoles some of our grandmothers and some of our grandfathers would mix all kinds of tonics and elixirs. And the folks would be happy to get them because they really worked. Down South New Orleans way.

4 ozs water

1-2 jigger whiskey (100 proof)

1 large lemon

1 tbsp honey

1 large mug

1 Pour water and whiskey into small saucepan.

2 Cut lemon in half and squeeze juice in pan.

3 Next cut halves into fourths and add to pan

4 Bring to a boil on medium heat.

5 Allow to boil for 1 minute.

6 Pour in mug and drink.

7 Be careful not to burn yourself.

8 Draw bath water as hot as you can stand it.

9 Soak but do not let water become warm.

10 Dry and dress for bed.

11 Jump in bed and cover-up.

12 As snug as a bug in a rug.

NEW ORLEANS APPETIZERS

In this section are some of the appetizers that graced the banquet tables when I was a little girl. And these yummy tastes are gracing New Orleans menus still today. New Orleans of old loved to celebrate and needless to say its people still do.

Bon Appetit!

STORY TIME "CREOLE FINGER SANDWICHES DELIGHT"

I had to tell a short story about the creole finger/tea sandwich. It was always a hit at the earlier social balls, weddings, anniversaries, graduations, and just about every celebration in New Orleans.

The spicy and savory blends of chicken, ham, roasted beef, turkey, and tuna would surely delight the taste buds. The different blends of seasons and spices added to their recipes would always keep your guest guessing as to what it is in it.

The grandmothers and the aunts were usually the ones who made the sandwiches for all of the family weddings. Yes, they would have the sliced ham, roasted beef, turkey, cheese, etc; but it was nothing like the tasty meat salad ones.

I am going to use the New Orleans term, "back in the days" this meant in the days when you were young, and what was done. Well, I am saying this to say, New Orleans had many social and pleasure clubs. Some were educational ones, charitable fundraising ones, and some were for just gathering together and have a good time. There were formal, informal, casual, summer, winter, and holiday balls. You name it New Orleans had it. And low and behold the delicious little tastes would grace just about every table.

The finger/tea sandwich should be small, thin, and crustless bread sandwiches. They should not be overstuffed with an abundance of fillings, but instead should be dainty and delicate. Fillings always need to be spicy, flavorful, and interesting. But by no means hot, spicy does not mean hot. The term finger sandwiches refer to tea sandwiches cut in a specific way and served on fancy trays and platters.

As children, we had our own little social and pleasure clubs. We would meet once a month on Saturdays, conduct business, collect our fifty-cent dues, adjoin and then we would eat. Our menu would consist of various types of finger sandwiches, chips, and dips, fruit punch. My mama would make a nice homemade cake to grace the table. Our business discussions were about what was going on at school, who was having the next waistline party, and what you are going to wear. I think we were into little girl gossip so cute and we loved it.

DEVILED EGGS - STUFFED EGGS

The Deviled egg is truly Creole, New Orleans, and Southern. Simple yet very much sort after at any party. I loved them as a child and I still love them today. I don't wait for parties, I just make and eat them any old time. Made with or without relish, have it your way. At any celebration, they will always the first to go. Garnish them with paprika or cayenne pepper.

1 doz eggs (hard boiled)

1 to 2 tbsp sweet radish

2 tbsp mayonnaise

1 tbsp yellow mustard

1/4 tsp black pepper

salt (to taste)

paprika/cayenne pepper (sparkle top)

Hard boil oil eggs in a large pot. Peel eggs than slice them in half. Remove the yolks. Put yokes in a mixing bowl. Place egg whites on a tray & sit aside. Add all ingredients to egg yolks except for salt, paprika/cayenne then mix. You are looking for a pasty consistency. Add salt to taste Using a small spoon to stuff your egg whites Sprinkle tops with paprika/cayenne pepper. Arrange on serving platter Garnish with parsley. For a larger get together just double or triple your recipe & you are set to go.

Yield: 24 halfs

CREOLE LIVER PATE'

Yield: 14-18 serving

If you are a fan of liver cheese you will love this little treat. Great on any style cracker. A nice dip for all your fun parties. Just sitting around watching movies or a game your friends will love it taste. A New Orleans treat for all of your menus. Simple yet good.

1 pound chicken liver/pork/ veal liver

1/3 cup green onions (minced)

1-2 cloves garlic (minced)

4 tbsp butter

1/4 cup cream

1 tsp brandy (optional)

1/8 tsp rosemary

1/8 tsp oregano

1/8 tsp black pepper

salt (to taste)

cayenne pepper (pinch to taste)

1 Trim tissue and fat from livers.

2 Melt 4 tbsp butter in saucepan low heat.

3 Saute' livers and onions in pan.

4 Let brown on both sides.

5 May turn down heat to allow livers to cook (6-8 mins).

6 Add garlic and stir (2-3 minutes).

7 Spoon livers into a food processor and add spices'.

8 Add cayenne pepper and salt to taste.

9 Now puree'.

10 Creole taste test.

11 May look loose but your pate' will firm in the fridge.

12 Serve with your choice of crackers or thin slices of toasted french bread.

SWEETISH MEATBALLS

No sweetish meatballs no party. Never had of a party with the balls. There are many types of sauces you can add to your meatball it is up to you. Sweet & Sour, Cheesy, BBQ, Italian just the name a few, every one of them is great. Homemade mini meatball there is nothing like them. Any occasion and any style sauce, as they say, it in New Orleans, "It's all good".

2 pounds ground beef

1 cup bread crumbs (plain)

3 eggs (beaten)

1/4-1/3 cup milk

2 cloves garlic (minced)

1 large yellow onion (minced)

3 sprigs fresh parsley (minced)

1/4 tsp basil

1/4 tsp sage

1/4 tsp cayenne pepper

1/4 tsp black pepper

salt (to taste)

Mix ground beef & all ingredients together in a large bowl. Row meat into balls Dust with flour. Fry in oil until golden on med heat then place on paper towels to drain. Or you can try baking them. Preheat oven to 350 degrees Place meatballs in a greased baking pan & bake until brown on both sides Remove from pan & drain Put your meatballs in your choice of hot dish or pot. Pour on your favorite sauce. Not one will be left.

Yield: 24 - 36 mini meatballs

NEW ORLEANS CRAB BALLS

Yield: 20 crab balls

Creole crab balls are the life of any occasion menu. Spicy and delicious they will always hit the spot and will send you guests back asking for more. In New Orleans, if you did not have crab balls as part of your menu you were not having a party. Crabs balls are like you in a commanding sentence. It is understood. It always there and it is a must on every menu. Made with fresh crabmeat, lots of seasons, and spices you can not have just one. Add your favorite homemade dipping sauce and you are good to go.

16 ounces of crab meat

1-2 cup bread crumbs (plain)

2-3 eggs

2 stalks green onion (minced)

2 clove garlic (minced)

1/4 bell pepper (minced)

2 sprigs parsley (minced)

1/2 stick butter (melted)

1/8 tsp thyme

1/8 tsp sage

1/4 tsp oregano

1/8 tsp black pepper

1/8 cayenne pepper

salt (to taste)

1/4 cup butter

1 cup oil (vegetable)

1. Place all seasoning with 1/2 stick butter in skillet.

2. Saute' until tender over low/medium heat.

3. Mix eggs and spices in a mixing bowl.

4. Next, add the crabmeat and mix.

5. Combine all ingredients together.

6. Creole taste test.

7. Mix and then shape into balls (1-2 inches).

8. Light dust with flour.

9. Fry crab balls in oil in a large skillet.

10. May add more oil to fry crab balls.

11. Cook until lightly browned on both sides (3-4 minutes).

12. Remove for pan and let drain.

13. Or you can

14. Place balls in buttered greased baking pan.

15. Bake at 350 degrees until brown on both sides.

16. Serve with your chance of dipping sauce.

CREOLE HOG HEAD CHEESE

Now tell me, who in New Orleans doesn't know about hog head cheese? In my old sixth ward neighborhood about everyone ate it. My mother did not make it but my Auntie Alice would bring my mother all kinds of handmade treats. Hog Head Cheese and Boudin Sausage were one of her favorites. My mama and my Auntie Alice would sit around the table where they laugh, talk, and enjoy their food. And low and behold here would come Auntie Bay through the front door. It would be on the three sisters sitting around the dining room table. Having fun enjoying each other company laughing, and talking. My Auntie Alice had a heart of gold and always brought enough for mama to share with their other sisters. Creoles are well noted for their cooking, baking, and homemade goods. One of the popular ones is definitely hog head cheese. One little tip is to always, always taste test your food. If you are not used to spicy food just cut back on the spices called for in the recipe. After taste testing, you can always add more to your dish. Remember you can add but you can not take away. this is a dish that calls for a lot of seasoning and spices. the more the merrier. Try it you may like it.

2-3 pork roast (shoulder)

2 pig feet (fresh & split)

1 gallon water

2 yellow onions (chopped)

3-4 green onions (chopped)

3 cloves garlic (minced)

2 stalk celery (chopped)

1/2 green bell pepper (chopped)

6 sprigs fresh parsley (chopped)

1/2 tsp oregano

1 tsp thyme

1/2 tsp sage

3 fresh bay leaves

2 pks gelatin (unflavored) (optional)

1 tsp cayenne pepper

1/2 tsp black pepper

1 tsp salt

Clean and rinse pork. Put all meat in a large stockpot. Add water enough to cover the meat. Add all spices. Cook on med heat. Bring to a boil. Cook until the meat becomes tender enough to easily be removed from the bones. Carefully remove all meat and bones from the pot. Let cool enough to handle. Separate all meat from the bones. Chop some of the pork and shred some with hands. The thickness of the chopped pork is your choice. Add all seasoning, meat, and remaining liquid to pot. At least 4 cups is needed. Cover and simmer, stir every 15-20 minutes to keep from sticking. Allow to cook for 3 hours on low-medium heat. Your dish should have the consistency of a stew. More water may be added while cooking. The unflavored gelatin mix may be added only if you need it. Creole taste test. Pour into a casserole dish or pan. Let chill until set 5-8 hours. Can be served on crackers, thin slices of toasted french bread, etc. The headcheese will keep for about a week. Remove bay leaves and strain the liquid in the pot to remove any more bones. Drain some of the greases from the liquid then return back to the pot. Add meat to liquid and simmer on low temperature for1/2 hour. Text taste for salt. Line pans with plastic wrap. Pour your hog head cheese into the pans. Set aside to cool before placing in refrigerate. The next day, un-mold the hog head cheese remove the plastic, and slice 1/2 in thick with a sharp knife. Can be served on crackers, thin slices of toasted french bread, etc. The headcheese will keep for a week.

Yield: cut in one inch slices

CREOLE OYSTER PATTIES

Yield: 24 servings

New Orleans oyster patties are a must-have on any and all occasions. From wedding to family reunions to the Mardi Gras balls, you are sure to see them gracing the banquet tables. Their spicey and savory filling make these little fellows one of the most sorts after appetizers on the most popular venue's menus in New Orleans.

2 doz puff pastry shells

1 quart oysters with liquid

1 large yellow onion (minced)

1 stalk green onions (minced)

2 cloves garlic (minced)

4 sprigs parsley (minced)

1/8 tsp thyme

1/8 tsp sage

1/8 oregano

1/8 rosemary

1/4 tsp black pepper

1/8 tsp cayenne pepper

salt (to taste)

1/4 cup flour

1/2 stick butter

1/2 cup whole milk or half & half

1 Drain oysters & save liquor.

2 Add butter to a saucepan.

3 Sauté onions & green onions until tender.

4 Mix the flour, half of the oyster liquid, and half of the milk.

5 Add to pan and stir well.

6 Let cook for (5-7 minutes).

7 Allow to thicken.

8 Chop oysters.

9 Add to the pan with all your spices.

10 Cook until oysters curl then add garlic and parsley.

11 May add the remainder of oyster liquid if needed.

12 Spoon oyster mixture into pastry shells.

13 Bake until brown at 350 degrees.

NEW ORLEANS SOUPS

Some of the delicious Creole-style soups that graced the family tables of New Orleans in my childhood days. Everyday soups you can still find in the restaurant's menus today.

MAMA'S SAVORY VEGETABLE SOUP

I don't know how my mother did it but she did. To the world, it is called the sixth sense but to me, I always know it was God moving in my mother's life. In my childhood days in New Orleans, we had winter, spring, summer, and fall. But I am here to tell you when the cold front shows her face, mama would somehow be ready for her. I would round the corner and the aroma of her soup would fill the air. Year after year she would make her vegetable soup on that first day of the cold front. She would have it ready for us when we came home from school. I would climb the front steps then on to the porch, into the house the aroma of her mouth warming soup would just draw me in. As I got to the kitchen I would just give my mother a big hug. No matter what the weather was like that morning if and when the cold front would hit mama was always ready with her delicious soup. She always would put oxtails in it. The pot would be huge because of her reputation in the family for her first day of winter soup. When you live in New Orleans or the surrounding areas of Louisiana you need all of the big pots you can get. We are people, who love good food, and Creoles love to share. Bon Appetit!

4-6 oxtails

1/2 stick butter

2 medium yellow onion (chopped)

1 green bell pepper (chopped)

4 stalks celery (chopped)

3 carrot (sliced)

4 cloves garlic (minced)

6 sprigs fresh parsley (chopped)

6 creole tomatoes (chopped)

1 small can tomato sauce

1/2 pound fresh green beans (sliced-1/2 pcs)

2 zucchini (diced) (optional)

1/2 cup corn

1/2 cup green peas

2 potatoes (diced)

1 tsp basil

1 tsp rosemary

1/4 tsp sage

1/2 tsp oregano

2 bay leaves

1/2 tsp black pepper

1/2 tsp cayenne pepper

1 tsp salt (to taste)

10 cups water

Rinse oxtails and season with salt. Place oxtails in small stockpot. Add 8 cups water and allow to cook until tender. Cut and prepare all other ingredients. Heat butter in a soup pot on medium-high heat. Add onion, celery, bell pepper, and carrot. Stir and let cook (5-7 minutes). Strain water from oxtails and add to the pot. Add garlic, spices, and all other vegetables except potatoes and zucchini. Add more water to have at least 10 cups of water in the soup pot and bring everything to a boil. Reduce heat to simmer, and cook uncovered. Add potatoes and zucchini. Simmer on low heat (30 minutes). Prepare your choice of pasta as directed on the package. Add to your pot. Cook vegetables are tender but not overcooked. Taste test for spices and salt add more if needed. Continue cooking another 10 minutes. Enjoy your soup as I did as a child and I still do today.

Yield: 10-12 servings

NEW ORLEANS OYSTER SOUP

This creole favorite is sure to be a hit and is sure to make the menu of many celebrations. It creamy and rich sauce is loved by many. For those of you who love oysters, this is the dish for you. Remember creole dishes is all about the seasoning and the spices. Cayenne is for adding a little spice to your dish. Try adding a pinch or two to some of your dishes and taste the difference for yourself.

2 qt oysters

3 stripes bacon (crumbled-optional)

1 lg yellow onion (chopped)

1 stalk green onion (chopped)

3 stalk celery (chopped)

2 sprig parsley (minced)

3 clove garlic (minced)

1/4 tsp thyme

1/4 tsp cayenne pepper

1 tsp white pepper

1/2 tsp salt

2 tbsp butter

1/2 cup flour (all-purpose)

2-3 cup milk (whole)

1 cup heavy cream

Fry the bacon until crisp (5-6 minutes). Place on paper towels and set aside. (optional) Allow 1/2 of fat from the bacon to remain in the pan. Add butter heat on medium. Add onions and celery saute stirring until soft (8-10minutes). Add the bacon, green onions, garlic, and spices to the pot. Add flour to the pot and stir. Continue stirring to make a light roux (3 minutes). Add the reserved oyster liquor and milk and bring to a boil. Reduce heat and simmer until the liquid thickens (5-8minutes). Add the oysters and simmer until the oysters start to curl (5-7minutes). Stir in the cream and cook another (3-5 minutes). Creole taste text. Remove from heat and adjust the spices to taste. Serve hot with thin slices of French bread. It's New Orleans delicious!

Yield: 8-12 servings

CRAB & CORN SOUP

This soup has a rich and smooth taste that most New Orleans people crave. Creole families have been cooking and enjoying this dish for decades. It has just enough seasonings and spices not to overpower the favor you are wanting it for...The Crab. A summer soup in a light sauce by adding more cream or a winter soup made thicker with less milk like chowder this dish is sure to please the plait. I guarantee. Creole Crab and Corn Soup is a much-loved dish in the New Orleans areas. I know it rang a bell in my sixth ward neighborhood. The photo in this recipe is my winter one. The taste is delightful.

8 ozs crabmeat

3-4 slices bacon (cut up) (optional)

1 large yellow onion (chopped)

1 stalk celery (chopped)

1 stalk green onion (minced)

2 sprigs parsley (minced)

1/2 cup butter

1/4 cup flour (all-purpose)

1 bay leaf (whole)

1/2 tsp rosemary

1/8 tsp thyme

1/8 tsp sage

1/8 tsp oregano

1/8 tsp cayenne pepper

1/2 tsp salt

1/8 tsp black pepper

1 can cream-style corn

1/2 can whole kernel corn (draine

2 cups irish potatoes (cubed & cooked)

2 cups milk (whole)

2 cups milk (half and half)

1/4 cup water

Place cut bacon in a saucepan and let cook but not until crisp. cut into tiny pieces and set aside. Add butter in a large saucepan over medium-low heat. Add onions and celery to the pan. Cook until onions are soft and translucent (6-10 minutes). Add flour into the sauteing mix. Add green onions, garlic, and parsley to the pan. Stir (6-8 minutes). Do not let brown. You are not making a roux. Next, add water stir while adding. Add all spices to the pan. Add crabmeat, bacon, corn, and potatoes to pan. Add 2 cups milk to the pan. Simmer on low/ med heat (30 minutes.). Add half and half to your dish. Cover and let cook another (30 minutes). Be careful not to let the soup stick/scorch. Do the creole taste test and make adjustments. May be garnished with more crab, cayenne pepper, and parsley.

Yield: 8 servings

CREOLE TURTLE SOUP

Be careful as to what you show or tell a child.
My daddy, my daddy's best friend, and my cousin Junior., my daddy's nephew decide to go fishing, and low and behold they came back with a live turtle. The three Musketeers is what I called them because of their beautiful friendship and family ties decided they were going to kill, clean, and cook the cowan/turtle for dinner that night. So they killed and cleaned their turtle. Then my daddy decided to give me a lesson on a turtle's heart. So he started by cut the heart in half the heart still beating, he cut the heart in fourths the heart was still beating. Next, he cut the heart into eights and the heart was still beating. At five or six years old that was a little bit too much for me. Out the backdoor, I flew. The three of them laugh and thought it was so fun. That night at dinner when my mother placed my plate in front of me, that was it. You could not tell me that turtle was dead. In my mind, it was still alive. And oh yes, it was time for me to break out the back door one more time. My mama came to my recure she said, "Charlie she is not going to eat it" and my daddy said, "fix her something else to eat". I had loving parents and they understood me, my expression said it all. As I grew older this little story became very funny to me. I thought this was another perfect time to tell it again. Those who know me have heard it from time to time and it just tickles my soul to share it again and again. Talking about the old days living in the sixth ward of New Orleans. Now back to the Turtle Soup it is one of the most sort after soups in the restaurants of New Orleans. It is rich and savory. Whether you make it with or without the brandy it is all good. I guarantee!

2 pounds turtle meat (diced

6 eggs (hard boil)

2-3 creole tomatoes (chopped)

2 yellow onions (chopped)

4 green onions (chopped)

4 cloves garlic (minced)

2 stalks celery (chopped)

1 green bell pepper

4 sprigs fresh parsley (minced)

3 bay leaves

1 tsp oregano

1/2 tsp thyme

1/8 tsp sage

1/8 tsp basil

1/2 rosemary

1 tbsp paprika

1/8 cayenne pepper

1/4 black pepper

1/2 tsp Salt (or to taste)

1 cup flour (all-purpose)

2 sticks butter

2 tbsp lemon juice (optional)

1/2 cup dry sherry (optional)

8 cups water

Washed and cleaned meat. Boil eggs and put aside. Place 1 stick butter in a large stockpot. Put meat in the pot along with heating butter. Add all spices to the pot. Let cook (20 minutes). Add the onions, green onions, celery, garlic, and bell peppers to the pot. Stir constantly. Saute until seasonings have caramelized (15-20 minutes). Add water and bring to a boil. Reduce to low heat. Simmer uncovered (30 minutes). Start to skim away any fat that develops at the top. Make a roux using flour and the other 1 stick of butter in a separate pot. Once the roux is ready, slowly add it to the soup. Let cook (30 minutes). Add tomatoes and continue cooking. Stir to prevent sticking. Add brandy and lemon juice to the pot (optional) Bring back to a simmer(20 minutes) Creole taste text. Let cook until the turtle is tender. Remove the soup from heat and serve. Add egg and garnish with parsley and cayenne pepper. Or let stand until soup reaches room temperature then refrigerate.

Yield: 10-12 servings

NEW ORLEANS YAKAMEIN

Everyone say hurray for Yakamein. This dish is true New Orleans. As a child growing up in the sixth ward of New Orleans, I can tell you some story about the very sought after Yakamein. The mama and pop restaurants, sweet shops, and lounges sold it. Yakamein was very delicious and the more cayenne pepper and green onions you put in it the better it tasted and it is for you. A great hangover remedy. After balls, dances, second lines, etc the New Orleans people are looking for the "Yak". I'll take a large one, please.

1-2 lbs beef (season, cook, and Chopped)

3 beef cubes

6 eggs

1 yellow onion (chopped)

1 stalk celery (chopped)

2 stalk green onions (chopped)

1/2 tsp thyme

1/2 tsp rosemary

1/2 tsp cayenne

1 tsp salt

2 beef cubes

1 pound spaghetti

Rinse and season roast. Cook beef 3 cups water, onions, and celery in a stockpot until tender. Set aside to cool then cut into cubes. Then again set aside. Boil egg (hard boil), peel, and place aside. Strain water from beef in a stockpot. Add other 3 cups water and bring to a boil. Add beef and beef cubes to the pot. Taste test for spices and adjust. Reduce heat and simmer and cook (45 minutes). Creole taste test. Cook the spaghetti noodles according to package directions. Put cooked spaghetti in a soup bowl. Can keep soup over low heat until needed. Serve in soup bowls using a slotted spoon. Add a boiled egg, either whole halved lengthwise. Spoon about 1 cup of the beef broth on top. Garnish with green onion and sprinkle cayenne pepper on top. the more green onions on top the merrier. You may add other ingredients such as shrimp, ham, and chicken.

Yield: 6-12 servings

SAVORY CHICKEN NOODLE SOUP

I would hear the neighborhood people say that chicken noodle soup was food for your stomach and food for your soul. All I know from a child it was so good. My daddy made it when he was home. My daddy was a merchant marine (seaman) and when daddy was home it was always a treat. He was a type of man you better not said "Daddy, Charley, Mr. Charley, Uncle Charley this is so good" because he would say "Have so more". As a young child, I would just marvel at the things my dad would do. The meals he would cook. His vegetable soup was so good that I did believe it was good for both the body and the soul.

4 roasted chicken breast (cut in cubes)

2 onion (yellow)

1 stalk green onion

2 garlic cloves (chopped)

2 stalks of celery (sliced)

4 sprigs fresh parsley (chopped)

2 carrot (sliced) (optional)

1 tsp rosemary

1/2 tsp thyme

1/4 tsp sage

1/2 tsp oregano

1 tsp paprika

2 bay leaves

4 tbsp butter

1/2 tsp cayenne pepper

1/2 tsp black pepper

1/2 tsp salt (to Taste)

8-9 cups water

1/2 pound pasta (your choice)

Season and roast chicken. Let cool and cut into cubes. Put butter in stockpot. Add onions, celery, carrots, and saute' (10 minutes). Next, add garlic, green onions. Continue to stir and let cook (5 minutes). Add parsley, chicken, and all spices to the pot. Continue to stir (2-4 minutes) add water. Taste test for spices and salt. Let cook (30 minutes) on med heat. Then allow to cook on low heat Cook until vegetables are tender. But not overcooked. Creole taste test again for spices. May add more water if needed. Next, drop in your cooked pasta of choice. Creole taste test. Simmer for (10-12 minutes). Enjoy!

Yield: 8-10 servings

DADDY'S SPLIT PEA SOUP

Yield: 8-10 servivgs

My dad would cook this dish for us. It was so so good. It had a great taste of ham, a little buttery, and all blended together with the split pea, I never had just one bowl. Split Pea Soup is easy to make and perfect for a cold winter day.

1 meaty ham bone (plenty meat on it)

1 pound green split peas

1 lg yellow onion (chopped)

2 stalk green onions (chopped)

2 cloves garlic (chopped fine)

3 stalks celery (chopped)

4 sprigs fresh parsley (minced)

1/4 tsp thyme

1/4 tsp oregano

1/2 tsp rosemary

2 bay leaves

cayenne pepper (pinch)

1/4 tsp black pepper

3 tbsp butter

8 cups water

1 Sort and rinse peas.

2 Put butter, onions, celery, and green onions in a stockpot.

3 Saute' on medium heat (10 minutes)

4 Add parsley and all spices to the pot.

5 Next, add water and ham bone.

6 Bring to a boil on medium heat.

7 Simmer on low heat (50 minutes)

8 Stir from time to time to keep from sticking.

9 Remove some of the ham from the bone and chop.

10 Add back to the pot.

11 Taste test for spices and salt.

12 More water may be added if need.

13 The slower it cooks the better it tastes.

14 Cook another 10 minutes.

15 Enjoy!!!

CREOLE STYLES SALADS

In this section are a sample of the many salads that was a part of my families everyday dinners. In days of old it was, "A salad a day keep the doctor away."

MAMA'S POTATO SALAD

Potato salad is the number one salad in the creole communities of New Orleans. The perfect side dish for just about everything. From fried chicken, fried seafood, it makes a great side for the baked dishes too. It is a hit in just about every restaurant in the city. When I was a little girl, I did not know too much about cold potato salad because it never lasted long enough to get to the frig. Cold or room temperature it is sure to lighten up your taste buds. For Sure. I love, love the this salad and I still make it all the time.

4 large Irish potatoes (peeled & cubed)

2 eggs (hard-boiled)

3 stalks green onion (finely chopped)

2 sprigs parsley (finely chopped)

2-3 tbsp yellow mustard

2 cup mayonnaise

2 tbsp vinegar

1/2 tsp black pepper

1/2 teaspoon salt (to taste)

Peel and rinse potatoes. Place cubed potatoes in a large pot. Fill with water and bring to a boil. After pot began to boil drop in eggs. Allow boiling until potatoes become soft. Remove from heat. Drain potatoes well. Peel eggs, chop, and put to the side. Place drained potatoes in a large mixing bowl. Add green onions and mix lightly. Next, add all other ingredients. Mix thoroughly and creole taste test (salt). Put your salad in a serving bowl. Can be served at room temperature. Or place in the refrigerator for later serving. This is all the ingredients I use for my salad. This is the ingredients my mother used. There is one difference my mother would mix the yolks and oil together before adding it to the salad. The secret to a good tasting salad is adding the green onions to the potatoes while they are still hot. And only use the green part of the green onions. This will give added flavor to your salad. Mama's salad was always a hit there were no leftovers. Try adding bacon bites or green olive when making this salad for your back your gatherings. It is sure to be a winner. add eggs, ceonion, pickle relish and juice into a large mixing bowl. Add half of the mustard and mayonnaise and stir well to combine. Add enough of remaining mixture to give the potato salad a creamy consistency, but not too wet. Add salt and pepper, adjusting to taste if needed. Refrigerate until ready to serve. The longer it sits, the more the flavors will meld together. Just before serving, sprinkle with paprika.

Yield: 6-8 servings

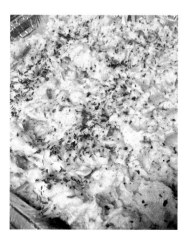

SPICY CREOLE OKRA SALAD

Yield: 6 servings

This is definitely a creole dish. As a little girl, I would see my mother, my Auntie Alice, and My Auntie Bay sitting around the dining table. The coffee would be flowing and the conversations would be in creole. Just sitting there enjoying their okra salad. Okra whether in a salad, fried, smothered, or in gumbo, it is one of the most sort after dishes in southern Louisiana. Don't knock it until you try it.

1 pound fresh okra	**1** Wash okra. remove tops and tips.
1 red onion (sliced thin)	**2** Place water in a medium saucepan.
2 cloves garlic	**3** Place okra in a pot with 1 tsp salt.
2 sprigs parsley	**4** Bring to a boil.
1/8 cup vinegar	**5** Let cook for (1 minute).
1/8 cup olive oil	**6** Drain, dry, and let cool.
1/4 tsp oregano	**7** Remove tops and tips.
1/2 tsp rosemary	**8** Cut okra diagonally or leave whole
1/8 tsp sage	**9** Add onion, garlic, and all other ingredients to the bowl. Toss.
1/4 tsp thyme	**10** Creole taste test.
black pepper & salt to taste	**11** Refrigerate for 30 minutes.
	12 You are ready to serve.

MACARONI SALAD

Macaroni salad is a good choice for outings and parties. Wondering what to do with your leftover pasta from making baked macaroni with meatballs in red gravy? It's the perfect salad to make and it is so easy. Not only those it taste good a little goes a long way. Just add in your choice of meat and you are good to go. Loved it as a child and as an adult I love this salad even more.

1/2 pound crab meat, shrimp, ham, or chicken (your choice)

1/2 pound elbow macaroni (cooked)

2 stalks green onions (finely chopped)

2 stalk celery (chopped)

1 cloves garlic (minced)

2 sprigs fresh parsley (finely chopped)

1 tsp paprika

1/4 tsp oregano

1/2 tsp rosemary

1/4 tsp thyme

1/4 tsp cayenne pepper

1/4 teaspoon black pepper

1/2 tsp salt

1 cups mayonnaise

3 tbsp yellow mustard

1 cup sour cream

salt to taste

2 tbsp butter or 1/4 cup vegetable oil

Bring a large pot of salted water to a boil. Add macaroni to pot and cook according to package directions. Rinse with cold water and let drain. Transfer to a large mixing bowl. Saute your choice of meat in butter or oil in a saucepan (10 minutes) on low heat. Add garlic to the pan. Add all ingredients including your choice of meat to the bowl. Mix thoroughly. Taste for spices, salt and adjust as needed. Made add more mayonnaise or 1/8 cup water if needed to loosen. Place in refrigerator or serve at room temperature.

Yield: 12 serving

CREOLE STYLE CABBAGE SALAD

From a child, I was always crazy about cabbage. This salad was a popular salad among the creoles in the area. My mother would make this salad for her sister, my Auntie Alice when she would come to visit us. She loved it and I did too. The blend of the cabbage and vegetables coupled with the sweet raisins does the trick for this salad. You can try dried cherries and dried cranberries in this too. A delightful taste and so easy to make. I have nicknamed this salad. I call it the Mardi Gras Salad because of its colors. An oldie but a goodie.

1/4 head green cabbage (shredded)

1/4 head red cabbage (shredded)

1 carrot (shredded)

3 sprigs fresh parsley (chopped)

1/2 red onion (shredded)

1/2 green bell pepper (shredded)

1 cup raisin

1/2 cup dried cherries (optional)

3 tbsp honey

1/4 cup vinegar

1/4 cup olive oil

2 tsp yellow mustard

2 tsp mayonnaise

1 tsp rosemary

1 tsp thyme

1/4 tsp cayenne pepper

1/4 tsp black pepper

salt to taste

Wash and dry all vegetables. Cut and prepare. Combine cabbage, carrots, parsley, onion, raisins, cherries, and bell pepper set aside. Combine sugar/honey, vinegar, oil, and mustard. Add mayonnaise and all spices. Add to salad and toss well. Creole taste test. Refrigerate until ready to serve.

Yield: 10-12 servings

FRESH SUMMER SALAD

A summer salad is the next best salad of choice after the popular potato salad. When you want to lighten up on your calories this is the one for you. I remember my mother salad bowl it was a very large crystal one and she had another one she uses for her potato salad. In the sixth and seventh ward of New Orleans, all of the ladies had one. Oh, please do not try to use them for something else, please don't. And that is the way it was growing up in my New Orleans neighborhood. A place for everything and everything in its place.

1 large head lettuce (your choice)

3 creole tomatoes or 1 pkg cherry tomatoes

1 small red onion (sliced thin)

2 cucumber (peeled and sliced)

1 green bell pepper (sliced thin)

1 carrot (shredded)

3 sprigs fresh parsley (minced)

1/2 pound ham (chopped) (optional)

1/4-1/2 pound cheese (shredded & your choice)

1/4 cup black olives

1/4 cup pickles (sliced)

1/2 tsp rosemary

1/2 tsp black pepper

Wash lettuce and spin dry. Tear into bite-size pieces. Wash all other vegetables. Slice tomatoes into wedges (8). Place all ingredients in a large bowl and toss. Refrigerate until ready to use. Garnish boil eggs halves. Make a nice light vinegarette dressing. Add your choice salad dressing right before serving.

Yield: 10-12 servings

SAVORY CHICKEN SALAD

Back in the days, our mamas made the best chicken salad. I remember mama would use the leftover breast from her bake hens, chickens, and rosters. The already season poultry added the special flavor needed for a savory tasting salad. For special occasions, the little old creoles lady would season and bake the chicken to make the salad. Not a one would be left on the trays.

6 breast or 1 whole chicken (seasoned and roast)

1 rib celery (chopped)

2 stalk green onion

1 clove garlic (minced)

3 sprigs fresh parsley (minced)

1/2-1 cup mayonnaise

1-2 tsp yellow mustard

1/4 tsp paprika

1/8 tsp cayenne pepper

1/8 tsp rosemary

1/8 tsp oregano

no black pepper (already in roasted chicken)

no salt (already in roasted chicken)

4 tbsp drippings from roasted chicken

Season and roast chicken. Set aside to let cool. Remove bones and chop. Place chicken in a medium-size mixing bowl. Add all seasonings, drippings, and spices. Toss lightly. Add mayonnaise and mustard. Mix thoroughly. Use for dips, party sandwiches, and vegetable trays. Itis sure to be a hit on any occasion.

Yield: 12-16 servings

SASSY TUNA SALAD

Yield: 10-12 servings

Whenever I see or taste tuna, I think of my childhood days and of the Lenten sessions of the church. From the tuna salads, tuna stuff tomatoes, and tuna casseroles as a child I enjoy them all. Tuna was a quick and easy lunch, dinner, or supper during the Lenten season. I still love tuna fish to this day. Oh please do not let me find some french bread. For there is nothing like a tuna on french dressed. And try adding some dried cranberries or cherries to your sandwich. You will be good to go.

4 can tuna (drain)

1 cup mayonnaise

2 tbsp sweet pickle (optional)

1 boiled egg (finely chopped) (optional)

1 stalk celery (chopped)

1 stalk green onion (minced)

1 clove garlic (minced)

1 tbsp yellow mustard

1/8 tsp thyme

cayenne pepper (pinch)

1/8 tsp black pepper

salt to taste

1 Place seasoning and spices in large mixing bowl.

2 Mix add mayonnaise, relish, and mustard.

3 Mix add chopped eggs.

4 Creole taste test.

5 Keep refrigerated until serving time.

6 Use for dips, party sandwiches, vegetable trays, etc.

7 Also great for stuffing tomatoes.

EGG SALAD- A LENTEN DELIGHT

I just have to say a little something about this sample little sandwich. As a child, I can remember eating it doing the Lenten season. It was quick, sample yet so very good filler upper. Sample yet good. Everyone in the 6th & 7th wards of New Orleans knows about this sample little sandwich. It was eaten a lot during the Lenten season. It would be a quick and easy go-between dinner. As you can see my sandwich is loaded with black pepper & mayonnaise (just the way I like it). Just a quick & easy treat for lunch or just a plain snack. Lagniappe (lan-yap) time...the secret to any style egg is black pepper. Hear me now it's the black pepper. In my New Orleans voice "ya heard me". A true lenten time snack!!!

3 eggs

2 tbsp mayonnaise

1 tsp yellow mustard

salt (pinch)

black pepper (pinch)

cayenne pepper (pinch-optional)

4 pieces bread (sliced-your choice)

Boil & peel eggs. Place in a small mixing bowl. Chop eggs. Add mayonnaise, mustard, salt, and black pepper. Mix together then spread on sliced bread. Add garnishing of your choice. Eat & Enjoy!

Yield: 2 sandwiches

SPICY TURKEY SALAD

Oh, remember the leftovers from the 20-22 pound turkeys from Thanksgiving and Christmas. Back in the days the bigger the turkey the better. What did our mamas do with them, especially the breast? Our mamas would make a salad and sometimes they would put it in soups. Don't forget baked turkeys made the best sandwiches for weddings and special occasions. Creole tea/finger sandwiches were at the top of the wedding's food menus. And the little old ladies of the neighborhood enjoyed making them. And we enjoyed eating them.

1/2 roasted turkey breast (chopped)

1 stalk celery (chopped)

1 stalk green onion (minced)

3 sprigs parsley (chopped)

1/2 cup green pitted olives (sliced) (optional)

1-2 cup mayonnaise

2 tbsp yellow mustard

1/8 tsp cayenne

1/8 basil

1/8 tsp cayenne pepper

no black pepper or salt

1/4 cup turkey gravy

1 Place chopped turkey In a large bowl.

2 Add all other ingredients to the bowl.

3 Can add 1/4 cup of leftover turkey gravy.

4 Mix well.

5 creole taste test for salt.

6 Try adding chopped nuts, or dried fruit, olives to your salad.

7 May serve right away or can be placed covered into the refrigerator. It is sure to please.

Yield: 10-12 servings

LASSEZ LES BONS TEMPS ROULER

In this section are the every days dish that our mamas cooked and serve to us as children. The Monday Red Beans, the Friday Fish Fries and Seafood Dinners. The Holiday Gumbas.

LET THE GOOD TIME ROLL!!!

CREOLE OKRA GUMBO

Here we go, people. One of the most favorite dishes in the south. Second only the Creole Style File' Gumbo. In my childhood day growing up in the sixth ward, it was the dish to die for. Okra Gumbo was considered the summer gumbo of the creoles in New Orleans. Rich in flavor and loaded with spices it was the choice of most summer Sunday dinner. We loved the seafood and the variety of meats and sausages our mothers and grandmothers used to put in it. I enjoyed eating this dish as a child and I still enjoy eating it today. The only thing different is now I am doing the cooking for my family and friends.

4 pounds fresh okra (sliced 1/2 inch)

4 pounds raw shrimps (deveined)

5 Louisiana blue crabs (broken in pieces)

1 pounds chicken (wings or small pieces)

1 pounds ham (cut small cubes)

1 pound smoked sausage (sliced)

1/2 pound hot sausage (make into tiny balls)

6 creole tomatoes (chopped) or 16 oz can of tomatoes

4 yellow onions (chopped)

6 green onion (chopped)

1 bell pepper (chopped)

6 sprigs fresh parsley (chopped)

1/2 tsp thyme

1/2 tsp sage

1 tsp oregano

1 tsp rosemary

3 bay leaves

1 tsp salt

1/2 tsp black pepper

1 tsp cayenne pepper

1/2 cup flour (all-purpose)

1 stick butter

1/3 cup flour (all-purpose)

6 qts water

Clean and prepare all meats and seafood. Rinse and cut all okra and seasonings. Cut off heads and tips from okra. In a large heavy stockpot add okra and 1/2 stick butter on medium heat. Let cook until okra starts drying out (20-30 minutes). You may turn down heat to keep okra from sticking or burning. Add onions and bell peppers. to pot. Allow to cook stirring constantly (10 minutes). Place pot aside. Add chicken, ham, and smoked sausage to another saucepan and allow to cook (15-20 minutes). Add green onions, parsley, and garlic. Add three quarts of water, tomatoes, and all spices. Place on low heat and allow to cook (1/2 hour). Stir occasionally to keep from sticking. Pour in the last three quarts of water. Meanwhile in a saucepan put remaining butter and flour for a roux. On medium heat stir and bring to a medium brown. Add hot sausage, shrimps, and crabs to your pot. Check the water level may add more if needed. Add okra, roux, and bring to a boil (20 minutes) Taste test for flavor and adjust spices accordingly. This recipe is for a big Sunday or Holiday pot of gumbo. Do not be afraid to cut this recipe in half. You can do it. Slowly add to your pot. Add hot sausage balls, parsley, and bring to a boil. Let cook cover over medium heat (15 minutes). Stir in shrimps, crabs, cover, and let cook. Check your water level in pot and if okra is cooked. The Creole taste test is very important for salt and spices. Away remember this is a spicy dish. the spicer the better. Serve with steamed white rice. This gumbo has the consistency of a rich soup so adjust your water as needed and your spices.

Yield: 15-18 servings

CREOLE STYLE FILE' GUMBO

Now, gumbo is like the King of Mardi Gras. The New Orleans Creole File' Gumbo. Can I get an amen, a "ya you right", a "you better say that", a "yes indeed"? Anyone will do when you are talking about gumbo. The aroma would fill the air in New Orleans neighborhoods. You were not having a holiday if you were no serving gumbo. Not in the sixth ward, not in New Orleans or the surrounding areas. I still remember the Thanksgivings and Christmas' we would have at my grandfather and grandmother's house out in the country. My Auntie Alice would grace the family with a huge pot of gumbo. It would be packed with, meat, sausage, shrimp, and crabs. So good and spicy. You could smell its aroma the minute we would turn off of the river road into the property lane. Oh, what a gathering it would be. Daddy would bake the ham and the huge turkey. He would also bake lemon meringue and apple pies for the family. And the love and excitement of the holidays just filled the air.

4 pounds raw shrimp (peeled & veined)

4-6 blue crabs (cleaned and in pieces)

1 pound seasoning ham

1 pound smoked sausage

1 pound hot sausage

2 pounds chicken wings (cut in threes)

1 pound gizzards (optional)

3 yellow onions (chopped)

4 cloves garlic (chopped)

5 stalks green onions (chopped)

1 green bell pepper (chopped)

1 tsp thyme

1 tsp oregano

1 tsp sage

2 tsp rosemary

1/2 tsp cayenne pepper

1/2 tsp black pepper

1 tsp salt

4 bay leaves

2/3 cup vegetable oil

1/2 cup flour (all-propose)

2 gals water

3 tbsp file'

Clean crabs and shrimp and put aside. Rinse shrimp shell and put in pot, add one gallon of water and bring to a boil. Let boil (20 minutes) and place pot aside. Cube ham and slice smoke sausage and place aside. Clean chicken pieces and put aside. Removed hot sausage from the casing & rolled into small balls and put aside. Clean gizzards, place in a small pot let boil until tender. Next, let cool, cut into pieces, and put aside. Heat oil and flour in a saucepan on medium heat for the roux. Stirring continually to prevent roux from burning. When your roux turns medium brown place aside. In a very large stockpot add one stick butter and chicken on medium heat. Allow to cook (30 minutes). Next add ham, smoked sausage, and all seasoning except parsley and garlic to pot. Allow to cook (30 minutes). Stirring continually to keep your pot from sticking. Strain shrimp shell from water and add to the pot. Next, add roux, gizzards, garlic, parsley, and bay leaves to the pot. Bring to a boil. Then add hot sausage, shrimps, and crabs. Add half of the remaining water to your pot. Allow to cook on medium-hot for half an hour. Do your creole taste text important. Add more salt, cayenne, spices if needed. May add remainder of water if needed. Remember File' Gumbo is a very spicy dish. Load it up. Cook on low fire for about 35 minutes. Add filé powder and stir into gumbo (optional). Many people prefer not to use file' in their gumbo. And some people prefer to sprinkle it in their individual bowls of gumbo. Either way File' Gumbo in the King and the Queen of Creole Cuisine. Serve over steamed rice and enjoy it.

Yield: 12-16 serving

SMOTHERED OKRA

Delicious and finger-licking good. A very spicy and full flavored dish. In the New Orleans language, "good eating". One of the number one dishes of creole families in the south. As a little girl I loved this dish and as an adult today I still cook smothered okra on those warm summer days when New Orleans comes to my mind. And when I think of those breezy summer days in the sixth ward back in the days!

2 lbs fresh okra (cut 1/2 inch slices)

2 pounds raw shrimp (cleaned and deveined)

1/2 pound ham (cut in cubes)

1/2 pound smoked sausage (cut in slices)

1/2 pound hot sausage (remove the casing and roll into tiny bite-size balls.

2 yellow onion (chopped)

4 stalk green onions (chopped)

1/2 green bell pepper(chopped)

4 cloves garlic (chopped)

4 sprigs parleys

1/2 tsp thyme

1/4 tsp sage

1 tsp rosemary

1/2 tsp oregano

2 bay leaves

1/2 tsp cayenne pepper

salt & pepper to taste

1/2 stick butter

2 cups water

Wash, dry, cut heads, and tips from okra. Next cut okra into 1/2 inch slices. Use a dutch oven. Heat butter over medium heat. Add okra to the pot. Cook on low heat (20-30 minutes). Or until okra starts drying out. Place pan aside. Saute ham and smoked sausage in another pan (10 minutes). Add onions and bell pepper to the pan. Continue to cook (10 minutes). Next, add the two pots together with all spices. Continue cooking on low heat(20-30 minutes). Add garlic and parsley to your pot. Add water one cup of water and bay leaves to the pan. Saute hot sausage (5 minutes) then add to the pan. Stir occasionally to keep from sticking or scorching. Add shrimps to the pot. Next, add the last cup of water if needed or more if needed. Cover and let cook (30-40 minutes) on low heat. Creole taste test. Add salt and spices to taste. Don't be afraid of the cayenne pepper for this is a noted spicy dish. Smothered Okra is a dish that is served over steamed rice.

Yield: 8-12 servings

MAMA'S RED BEANS WITH RICE

Hello, somebody! Now, who doesn't about and love New Orleans Creole Style Red Beans? Served over steamed rice is, sure enough, aimed to please. The people of New Orleans back in the days seasoned their beans with a choice of pickled meats (pickled tips, pickled pigtails), ham hocks, and ham. No smoke sausage in their beans back in the days. That came along a lot later. When we wanted a smoke flavor we chose smoked neck bones and smoked ham hock. And still, today when I wanted the true taste of New Orleans I know just what to do. I know how to www.neworleansmeat market/sendit quick.com. Ha Ha Ha

1 pound kidney beans

1-2 pound seasoning meat

1 large yellow onion (chopped)

2 stalks green onions (chopped)

3 clove garlic

1/4 bell pepper

2 sprigs parsley

2 stalk green onions (chopped)

1 stalk celery (chopped)

1 bay leaf

1/2 tsp oregano

1/8 tsp sage

1/8 tsp thyme

1/4 tsp rosemary

salt (to taste)

black pepper

10-12 cups water

Rinse beans and put beans in a medium-size bowl. Cover with water, cover, and place in the refrigerator. Let soak overnight this is called "soaking your beans". Next day drain beans and set aside. In a large pot, put one stick butter along with seasoning meat on medium heat. Let cook stirring (15 minutes). Add onions, bell pepper, and celery continue to let cook (10 Minutes). Add green onions, parsley, garlic, and all spices to the pot. Continue to let cook (5 minutes). Next, add drained kidney beans and 10 cups of water. Stir and bring to a boil. Reduce the heat to medium-low and simmer, uncovered. Stir occasionally and let cook until meat and beans become tender and bean gravy starts to thicken (60 minutes). This is called creaming. Add more water a cup at a time. With the back of a heavy spoon, mash about 1/4 of the beans against the side of the pot. Continue to let cook on low heat until the beans are tender and creamy (45 minutes). The creole method of soaking the beans overnight along with the adding of the butter to the dish adds in the creaming of your beans. Taste test and adjust. remember to remove bay leave afore serving. New Orleans Red Beans is always served over rice. It is never mixed together.

Yield: 8-10 serves

SIXTH WARD WHITE BEANS

The kidney beans are the number one bean in creole cooking and next is the northern, the white bean. And most of your beans are all cooked the same way. The difference is in the timing. Some will take longer to cook than others. Some of the names of the other beans dish popular in New Orleans are butter beans, northern beans, black beans, and black eye peas. Whichever one they are all good when seasoned the New Orleans way. Like my Auntie Alice use to say, good eating.

2 pounds seasoning meat (your choice)

1 pound dried navy beans

1 yellow onion (chopped)

2 stalks green onion (chopped)

2 stalk celery (chopped)

1/4 green bell peppers (chopped)

3 clove garlic (minced)

2 bay leaves

1/2 tsp rosemary

1/8 tsp sage

1/4 tsp oregano

1/8 tsp thyme

1/2 tsp black pepper

1/2 tsp salt

1 stick butter

10 cups water

Rinse beans and put beans in a medium-size bowl. Cover with water, cover, and place in the refrigerator. Let soak overnight this is called "soaking your beans". Next day drain beans and set aside. In a large pot, put one stick butter along with seasoning meat on medium heat. Let cook stirring (15 minutes). Add onions, bell pepper, and celery continue to let cook (10 Minutes). Add green onions, parsley, garlic, and all spices to the pot. Continue to let cook (5 minutes). Next, add drained white beans and 10 cups of water. Stir and bring to a boil. Reduce the heat to medium-low and simmer, uncovered. Stir occasionally and let cook until meat and beans become tender and bean gravy starts to thicken (45 minutes). This is called creaming. Add more water a cup at a time. With the back of a heavy spoon, mash about 1/4 of the beans against the side of the pot. Continue to let cook on low heat until the beans are tender and creamy (40 minutes). The creole method of soaking the beans overnight along with the adding of the butter to the dish adds to the creaminess of your beans. Taste test and adjust. remember to remove bay leave afore serving. New Orleans Red Beans is always served over rice. It is never mixed together.

Yield: 8 serves

BAKED TURKEY

Who doesn't love baked turkey? My daddy baked the biggest, tastiest, juiciest turkeys you would want to eat. Daddy's turkey would have the caps and nothing under twenty-three pounds for my daddy. He would have enough for all. The one in this picture is a 14-pound one and it was baked for oyster dressing once it is taken out of the oven like my mother used to do. Mama would bake her turkeys, remove it from the oven, stuff it with oyster dressing, and then place it back in the oven. When mama stuffed her turkey with the creole traditional dressing she stuffed the bird and lace it up, then into the oven, it would go. Whether unstuff daddy style or stuffed mama style, as we say in NewOrleans, "It's All Good".

1 turkey 14-16 lbs. (or larger your choice)

1 sticks butter

2 large yellow onion (cut in 1/8s)

1/2 large bell pepper (chopped)

3 stalks celery (chop in 1 inch pcs.)

2 garlic cloves (minced)

2 tsp paprika

salt (to taste)

1 tsp black pepper

cayenne pepper (pinch)

1-2 tsp rosemary

1/2 tsp thyme

1 cup water

Remove neck, gizzards, and livers from cavity. Rinse the turkey and pat dry. Rub the body of the turkey with all of the spices. Use extra spices to season the cavity. Place the turkey in a large deep roasting pan. Place pieces of onions, bell pepper, garlic, and celery in the cavity. Place the rest of the seasoning around turkey in pan. Put 1/2 stick of butter in cavity and other 1/2 stick in pan. Preheat the oven to 400° Roast the turkey at this temperature (30minutes). Then lower the heat to 350°. Roast for about 3-3 1/2 hours. Base often cavity and outside of your turkey. Bake until the juices run clear. Remove from the oven and let cool for 10 minutes. Lift the turkey out of the pan and carve. Strain gravy and taste test. Pour in saucepan and bring to a boil. May add 1-2 tbsp of flour to 1/4 cup water. Stir and pour into saucepan to thicken gravy.

Yield: 12-15 lbs. serves 10-12; 15-18 lbs. / 14-16; 18-22 lbs. / 20-22

BAKED DUCK

Yield: 8-14 servings

Roasted duck was a added treat to any holiday menu.
When my daddy would be home from Christmas he have roasted duck with all of its triming of orange
and aparcot sauce. From my childhood days untill today everyone that knows me know that this is one
of my favorite dishes. It is part of my Christmas menu just like my daddy. Served with one of the many
creole side dishes you can not lose with your guest who coming for Christmas or Thanksgiving.
I have roasted duck and baked ham every Christmas. My daddy and my mama would have the baked turkey adding to their
menu. And the gumbo was like you in a commanding sentence, it was understood it was going to be there on the menu.
If you are having family over for dinner you may want to serve 3 ducks.

2 ducks (5 pounds each)

1/2 yellow onion per duck

1 tsp rosemary per duck

1 tsp paprika per duck

1/2 tsp thyme per duck

1/4 tsp black pepper per duck

cayenne pepper (pinch)

1/2 tsp salt per duck

1/2 tsp black pepper

1. Clean and wash duck.

2. Dry. inside and out.

3. Rub inside and out with spices.

4. Place a few pieces of seasoning in the cavity of duck.

5. Add 1/2 cup water per duck.

6. Set oven temperature at 400 degrees.

7. Place ducks in the oven.

8. Allow baking from (45 minutes).

9. Base duck and lower oven to 350 degrees.

10. Bake loosely tented with aluminum foil (1-2 hours).

11. Remove aluminum tent to finish browning.

12. Test meat for tenderness and when the juice runs clear your ducks are ready.

13. Remove from the oven and place on a decorative platter.

14. Garnish with cooked apricot half and parsley.

15. When serving duck dribble with apricot sauce.

MAMA'S BAKED HEN

I am going with my Auntie Alice saying, "Maglett Good Eating". In my sixth ward community, this dish was one of the Sunday dinner delights. Along with the much sort after Creole stewed chicken. Made with a stewing hen for a richer depth of flavor. A deep poultry flavor coupled with the richness of its gravy is sure to keep your family and friend coming back for more.

1 (4-5 pounds) hen

2 lg yellow onion (chopped)

2 stalks celery (chopped)

2 cloves garlic (chopped)

1 tsp rosemary

2 tsp paprika

1 tsp oregano

salt and black pepper to taste

cayenne pepper (pinch)

1/2 cup butter

1 cup water

Clean and wash hen. Preheat oven to 350 degrees. Place hen in a roasting pan. Season generously inside and out with spices. Add a small amount of seasonings into the cavity. Place 3 tablespoons butter in the hen cavity. Place the remaining seasoning around the bird in the pan. Arrange remaining butter around the hen exterior and add water Bake (90 minutes). Baste the bird with drippings. Continue to bake until your hen is tender and juice is clear. Remove hen from oven and taste test gravy. Remove hen from pan and strain gravy. Pour gravy into a small saucepan. Add 1 tbsp flour and 1/4 cup water to the pan. allow cooking until thickened. Cover hen with aluminum foil, and allow to rest about 30 minutes before serving. Serve with one of your favorite side dishes. Choose one from me book are have one of your own.

Yield: 6-8 serves

BAKED CORNISH HEN

Yield: 4 to 8 servings

My daddy would bake these little yummies. Whether he would slip them and brush them drown with butter, herbs, and spices or stuffed with wild rice dressing they were sure to please the plait. You do not have to do much to cornish hens. They have an appetizing taste of their own and serves great at any Sunday brunch or any dinner party.

4 Cornish hens

1/2 yellow onion (cut into 1/4)

1 glove garlic (cut in 1/4)

1 tsp rosemary

1 tsp paprika

1/4 black pepper

cayenne pepper (pinch)

4 tbsp butter

1/4 cup water

1 Wash and dry hens.

2 Place hens in a roasting pan.

3 Preheat oven to 350 degrees.

4 Rib with spices inside and outside.

5 Put 1/4 onion, 1/4 garlic, and 1 tbsp butter in each hen.

6 Cover tightly with foil.

7 May add water 1/8 cup at a time.

8 Bake (45 minutes).

9 Remove foil and return to oven until golden.

10 May take another (15-20 minutes).

11 Can stuff with a wild rice dressing and try legs with kitchen string. Either way, stuffed or unstuffed they are sure to please family and friends.

DADDY'S BAKED HAM

When I was a little girl, could hardly wait for the holidays to begin. The New Orleans holidays started from Thanksgiving on. There would be one thing I could be sure of was my daddy's beautiful decorated ham. there it would be gracing the holiday table. With cherries, pineapples, and all of it cloves it was a sight to see. Daddy would bake a whole ham and the bigger the better was the way he saw it. But needless the say our family needed a whole one to accommodate all of our family and friends that would come by to say Happy Thanksgiving or Merry Christmas. My father and mother would welcome them all for they always have enough for everyone. the one in this photo was baked and the cherries will be placed on it later and replace in the oven not to burn them. I still bake whole ham until today. It was for a Christmas party is the reason it was in two pieces. Easyer to crave.

1 (10 – 12 pound) whole ham (fully cooked)

1 (20 oz) can pineapple rings (reserved juice)

1 cup packed brown sugar

1 cup 7-Up

whole cloves

1 10 oz jar maraschino cherries

1/3 cup honey

1/4 cup flour

1 tsp lemon juice

1 tsp oregano

2 tbsp rosemary

Toothpicks

Preheat oven to 350 degrees. Place oven rack on the lowest position in oven. Remove all other racks from oven. Add a roasting rack to the roasting pan. Mix brown sugar, 7-Up, honey, lemon juice, oregano, and rosemary in a small saucepan on medium heat. Let cook (5 minutes) until thicken then set aside. Remove all skin from your ham. Score, run a chef's knife diagonally across ham (one-two inch cuts). Turn ham and cut diagonally across it in the opposite direction, creating a diamond-shaped pattern over the surface of your ham. Place the prepared ham cut-side up in pan. Brush half of the prepared ham glaze over the surface of ham and bake (90 minutes). Remove ham from the oven, arrange pineapple rings over the top securing each slice with toothpicks. Place whole cloves in intersections on ham. Secure cherries in the center of pineapple with a toothpick. Brush half of the remaining glaze over the ham, covering the pineapple and cherries as well. Return the ham to oven and bake for an additional (30 minutes). Allow the ham to rest for 20 minutes, then remove cloves and toothpicks before carving. Let the ham rest for at least 10 minutes before slicing. This is my daddy's baked ham, it was so delicious and so beautiful to behold.

Yield: 18-20 servings

BAKED BUTT PORK ROAST

Sixth ward pork roasts were to die for. And my mother was noted for her three types of roasts. I enjoyed them so that I decided to put all three of her roasts in my book. They made great Sunday dinners. And what is a great side dish for any kind of pork dish are sweet potatoes/yams. The secret of good-tasting pork roasts is the garlic. Stuff, stuff, stuff.

5-6 Pork Roast (butt)

2 yellow onion (cut in 1/8)

1 stalks celery (chopped)

2 cloves garlic (sliced lengthwise)

1 clove garlic (chopped)

2 bay leaves

1 tsp rosemary

1/2 tsp oregano

1 tsp paprika

1/2 tsp sage

1/8 cayenne pepper

1/4 black pepper

1 tsp salt

1 tbsp heaping flour

2-3 cups water

lean and wash roast. Preheat oven to 350 degrees. Make deep incisions all over your roast. Mix the garlic cut lengthwise with 1/2 tsp salt, 1/8 tsp black pepper, 1/2 tsp paprika, 1/4 tsp oregano, and 1/4 tsp sage and insert into your roast. Mix the remainder of spices together and rub over roast. Place roast in baking pan. Place all seasonings in baking pan. Add water to the pan, one cup at a time. Bake uncovered until browned (60 minutes). After browning cover and continue cooking (2-3 hours) or until roast is tender. Base roast from time to time. After the roast is done, remove from pan and place serving plate. Strain gravy and pour into saucepan. Skim off any excess fat and thicken the drippings with a mixture of water, 2 tbsp butter, and flour. Allow cooking until gravy thickens. Taste test for spices and salt. May add another pinch of cayenne pepper.

Yield: 10-12 servings

MAMA'S SHOULDER PORK ROAST

This by far is my favorite cut of pork. Creole-style pork roasts are always rich in flavor and spices. And remember garlic is the key. I love the fact that pork roast leftovers are even better than the roast. Don't be afraid to load it up. As we would say in New Orleans, "put your foot in it".

7-9 pounds pork roast (shoulder)

2 large yellow onion (coarsely chopped)

3 cloves garlic (cut lengthwise)

2 cloves garlic Chopped)

1 tsp thyme

1 tsp rosemary

1 tsp oregano

1/2 tsp sage

2 tsp paprika

1/8 cayenne pepper

1/4 tsp black pepper

1 tsp salt

1/4 cup flour (all-purpose)

1/4 cup butter

3-4 cups water

Clean and prepare roast. Preheat oven to 350 degrees. You can cut about 3-4 slices across skin. of roast. Make deep incisions all over your roast. Mix the garlic cut lengthwise with 1/2 tsp salt, 1/8 tsp black pepper, 1/2 tsp thyme, 1 tsp paprika, 1/2 tsp oregano, and 1/4 tsp sage and insert into your roast. Mix the remainder of spices together and rub over roast. Place roast in baking pan. Surround roast with onions and garlic. Add water to pan, two cups at first. the rest as needed. Bake uncovered until browned on both sides (90 minutes). After browning cover loosely using an aluminum tent. Continue cooking (2-3 hours) or until roast is tender. Base roast from time to time and check the water level. After the roast is done, remove from pan and place serving plate. Strain gravy and pour into saucepan. Skim off any excess fat and thicken the drippings with a mixture of water, 1/4 cup butter, and flour. Allow cooking until gravy thickens. Taste test for spices and salt adjust.

Yield: 8-10 servings

MAMA'S POT ROAST

This creole favorite is a meal all by itself. Loaded down with tons of potatoes, carrot, and seasonings it is sure to please your taste buds. You can enjoy this dish in a bowl all by itself of you can drape it over hot steamed rice. Served with a nice salad and you are good to go. Mama's pot roast was a sure thing to a delicious heart meal.

4-5 pound pork roast (butt)

3-4 Irish potatoes (peeled and cut in 1/4s)

4-5 carrots sliced (optional)

2 yellow onions (chopped)

3 stalks green onions (chopped)

2 garlic (sliced lengthwise)

2 garlic (chopped)

4 sprigs fresh parsley (minced)

1/2 tsp thyme

1/2 tsp basil

1 tsp rosemary

1 tsp oregano

1 tsp paprika

1/4 tsp sage

1/4black pepper

cayenne pepper (pinch)

1 tsp salt

1/4 cup flour

3-4 cups water

1/2 stick butter

Clean and prepare your roast. Can be cook on top of the stove in a dutch oven or baked in a deep roasting oven. Preheat oven to 350 degrees. Stuff roast with sliced garlic, 1 tsp paprika, 1/2 tsp salt, and 1/4 tsp black pepper. Rub the remainder of spies on your roast. Place roast in baking pan. Add all seasonings in the pan. Add 1 cup of water. Place roast in oven and allow it to brown on both sides. Add potatoes and carrots to the pan. Add another cup of water. Cover lightly with foil and allow to cook until roast is tender. Baste meat and vegetables from time to time. Make a small roux with flour and butter and add to gravy. Taste test and adjust with spices and salt. May add another pinch of cayenne pepper to enhance the flavor of your dish.

Yield: 6 to 8 servings

BEEF RUMP ROAST

The best of both worlds mama did it her way and daddy did it his way either way it was good, good. A creole style rump roast loaded with spices is always delicious. As a little girl, I loved this type of roast severed with stream rice or baked potatoes, gravy, and my all-time favorite potato salad. Don't forget my green peas, yes peas. I loved them.

4-7 lb beef rump roast

2 yellow onions (cut in 1/8)

3 garlic (minced)

1/4 tsp oregano

1/2 tsp paprika

1 tsp rosemary

1/4 tsp thyme

1/8 tsp cayenne

1/4 tsp black pepper

1 tsp salt

1/4 cup flour (all-purpose)

3 tbsp butter

2 cups water

tsp salt

tsp black pepper

clove garlic

Preheat oven to 350 degrees. Prepare meat by rinsing and patting dry. Mix all of the spices together. Rub over roast. Place roast in a roasting pan. Allow roast to brown on both sides. Add onions and garlic to the pan. Add water to the pan. Let cook (90-120 minutes) tenting loosely with foil. Allow to cook until the temperature reaches 155 degrees. Next, add butter and flour to a small saucepan. Place on medium-high heat and mix a roux. Place roux aside. Next, when your roast is finished remove it from the pan. Remove all dripping and onions from the pan. Add to a small pot to make gravy. Add roux to the pot and allow to boil. Taste test and strain. Making a gray is optional for the dish.

Yield: 8-10 serving

CHUCK ROAST

As a little girl growing in New Orleans, I always enjoyed going to Kenner, Louisiana with my daddy. Daddy was a family man and a seaman and he would drive out Kenner to the slaughterhouses. There he ordered his beef by the half beef. I thought it was so exciting to see all of the slabs of beef hanging there in the huge freezers. I would run around trying to help my dad pick out a side of beef. Every once in a while my dad would say yes to the one I would pick out. Of course, it would make my day. Daddy would let the butchers know how he wanted it. And I would be adding in my two cents.

5-6 pound beef chuck roast (bone-in or boneless)

2 yellow onions (chopped)

3 cloves garlic (chopped)

1/2 bell pepper (chopped)

4 sprigs parsley (minced)

1/4 tsp sage

1 tsp oregano

1 tsp rosemary

1/8 tsp thyme

2 bay leaves

1/2 tsp black pepper

1 tsp salt (or to taste)

4 tbsp butter

1/4 cup flour (all-purpose)

3 cups water

This dish can be cooked on the stove in a dutch oven or in the oven. It is your choice. Clean and wash roast. Mix all spaces except for bay leaf. Next rub all over your roast. Add 2 tbsp butter. Place in a dutch oven or in roast pan. If on top stove heat at medium. If in the oven preheat oven 350 degrees. Let brown on both sides. Use flour and butter to make a roux in a small saucepan. Add all seasoning to roast. Add your bay leaves, roux, and water to roast. Cover lightly with foil. Let cook until tender. Taste test for spices and salt.

Yield: 8 servings

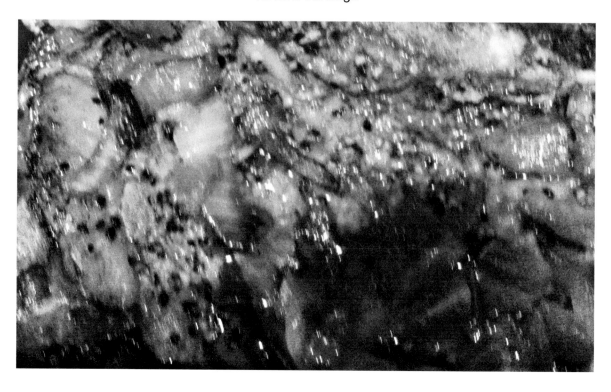

COD FISH PATTIES

People I must say during my nursey days in school this dish was a no, no for me. It was something about it, I just didn't look. Then about third grade, my dad asked me this question. Have you tried tasting it? I replied, "no I don't like it, I don't like the way it looks". And why would mama cook something like this for people? My daddy just laughed at me. Then daddy said why don't you try a little piece. So I did and low and behold I liked it. A true Lenten dish in the sixth ward. Until this day I still enjoy eating it.

1-2 lb codfish

2 -3 Irish potatoes

1 small yellow onion (chopped fine)

1 stalk green onion (chopped fine)

2 sprigs parsley (minced)

2 cloves garlic (minced)

2 eggs, lightly beaten

1 cup bread crumbs

2/3 cup flour (all-purpose)

1/2 tsp oregano

1/2 tsp basil

1/4 tsp cayenne pepper

1 teaspoon salt

1/2 teaspoon pepper

1 cup vegetable oil

Boil and mash the potatoes set them aside. Season and bake the codfish until it flakes easily. Drain potatoes and flake the fish with a fork. Be sure to remove all bones. Mix fish, potatoes, and all other ingredients together. If too crumbly, add another egg. If too sticky, add some more bread crumbs. Form mixture into cakes and dust lightly with flour. Let fry on medium-low heat in oil until golden brown on both sides.

Yield: 6-8 serves

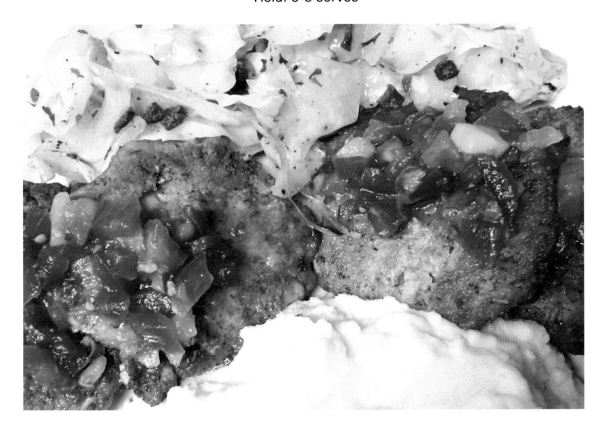

CREOLE STYLE BAKED RED FISH

I must say this is an oldie but goodie for me. I would get so excited when my mother would cook this one. From the well season fish to the rich and savory red sauce to it bring spooned over steamed rice, I was in seventh heaven with the taste. For you baked fish loves, I recommend this one. Its sure to please.

True creole cuisine at its best.

1 lg whole redfish (cleaned and trimmed)

3 cloves garlic (minced)

1/8 tsp rosemary

1/4 tsp thyme

1/4 tsp oregano

1/4 tsp cayenne

1/4 tsp black pepper

1 tsp salt

3 tbsp butter

1-2 Lemon (thinly sliced)

Red Sauce

3 cans tomato sauce

1 yellow onion (chopped)

2 stalk green onion (chopped)

1/2 bell pepper (green)

1 stalk celery (chopped)

3 sprig parsley (chopped)

1 bay leave

1/8 tsp thyme

1/4 tsp oregano

1/8 tsp sage

1 tsp rosemary

1/4 tsp black pepper

cayenne (pinch)

1/2 tsp salt

1 tsp sugar

1/4 flour (all-purpose)

1/4 cup vegetable oil

Preheat oven to 350 degrees. Wash the fish and dry on paper towels. Score both sides of fish about 3 times. Mix garlic and rosemary together. Put mixture inside each of the 6 cuts on the fish. Mix all other spice together. Rub all over your fish. Spread baking pan with 3 tbsp butter. Place fish in pan and place in oven. Allow baking (20-30 minutes). Line fish with lemon slices. Dribble fish with red sauce. Place back in the oven and bake until done (20-30 minutes). We serve this dish with steamed rice. Garnish with parsley, lemon slices, and a generous helping of the Creole Red Sauce. Red Sauce Heat the oil in a large skillet over medium heat. Add the onion, bell peppers, and celery. Saute until tender. Put flour and butter in small saucepan on medium. Make a roux and set aside. Add the green onion, garlic, parsley cook (4 minutes). Add roux, tomatoes plus one can of water per can, sugar, bay leaves, thyme, all spices. Bring to a boil. Reduce to a simmer and cook (45 minutes). Stir to keep from sticking and taste test. Adjust spices and enjoy.

Yield: 6-8 serving

COUVILLION-CREOLE STYLE FISH STEW

Back in the days, the original Couvillion was made with fish heads (not catfish heads). My mama made her Couvillion using cut-up fish. She preferred catfish because of her children, fewer bones. Now using catfish in this dish has become the norm. Mama always made this dish with brown gravy and she used a medium brown roux. It was always quite savory and seasoned just right. The sixth and seventh wards had it going on with this spicy one. You go grandmas and mamas for keeping Creole Cuisine going and for keeping it real. And hats off to all you Creole out there who still keep it going on today. Let me not forget the papas and dads. When a Louisiana man can cook, he not only cooks he puts his foot in it. For sure!

3-4 catfish fillets (cut into large pieces)

2 yellow onions (chopped)

4 stalks green onions (chopped)

1/2 green bell peppers (chopped)

3 clove garlic (minced)

4 sprigs fresh parsley (chopped)

1 bay leaf

1/4 tsp thyme

1/8 tsp sage

1/2 tsp rosemary

1/4 tsp oregano

1/2 tsp paprika

1/2 tsp cayenne pepper

1/4 tsp black pepper

1/2 tsp salt

1/2 cup butter

1/2 cup flour

4 cups water

Prepare fish. Rinse, pat dry, and put aside. Put butter and flour in a large saucepan on medium heat. Allow to cook (7-10 minutes) to make a medium-colored roux. Next, add the onions and bell peppers, and to sauté (5 minutes). Reduce heat and add the bay leaf, garlic, parsley, and all spices to the pan. Allow to cook (3-5 minutes). Add water and bring to a boil. Allow to boil (2-4 minutes) Cover and let cook (25-30 minutes)on low heat. Taste test the gravy for salt and other spices, add accordingly. Cook (5 Minutes) then, add fish to the pan. Let fish cook covered (20-25 minutes) or until fish is tender and cooked. Couvillion is always served with steamed rice. Garnished with cayenne/paprika and green onion/parsley. Try a few slices of buttery French bread with your meal. You can't go wrong with this one.

Yield: 6 to 8 servings

NEW ORLEANS FRIED FISH

When I was a little girl, I remember fried fish was one of the most sort after meals for the Lenten season, for the Friday Night fish fries, and for the neighborhood weekend suppers. Some of the other choices of fish at those types of gatherings were speckled trout, rainbow trout, and red snipper. I have to say it again. Creoles people of Louisiana love good food and we love to share. Yes, we will look for a reason yes any reason to celebrate with family and friends. Potato salad was always the side dish and plenty of it. Fried fish and potato salad went hand and hand back in the days. And needless to say, they go hand and hand still today.

Eat up, people!

4 catfish fillets

1 cup cornmeal

1/4 cup flour (all-purpose)

2 eggs

1/8 cup buttermilk

1/8 tsp black pepper

1/4 tsp paprika

1/8 cayenne pepper

1/2 tsp salt

3 cups vegetable

Wash and pat dry fish. Sprinkle with salt and pepper to taste. Pour oil into a large frying pan on medium-high heat. Mix buttermilk, eggs, mustard, and all other ingredients together and set aside. Add the mixture to your fish and coat well. Roll in cornflour mix. Carefully add fish to the pan. Fry 1-2 filets at a time. Fry on both sides (4-6 minutes) and your fish is golden brown. Remove from pan and let drain on paper towels.

Yield: 4-8 serves

NEW ORLEANS FRIED SHRIMP

Another craving of New Orleans is the Creole style fried shrimp. Whether sitting up high on a seafood platter or on a shrimp po-boy sandwich these babies are sure to please. The shrimp has always been in high demand. We love shrimp, what I should say is Creoles love seafood. And we find all kinds of ways to cook it. Whether in gumbos, stews, boiled, stuffings, or just sauteed and put over rice Shrimp is a winner. Let me ask this question, "who can resist the mouth-watering taste of fried shrimp served with a side of potato salad. Who??? Back in the days straight from out of the Gulf and prepare, fresh shrimps were to die for!!!

2 pounds large raw shrimp (deveined)

2 large egg

1 tbsp yellow mustard

1/2 tsp oregano

1/4 tsp garlic powder

1/4 tsp cayenne pepper

1/4 tsp black pepper

1/2 tsp salt

1 cup yellow cornmeal

1/2 cup flour (all-purpose)

2-3 cups vegetable oil

Clean and drain shrimps. Leave tail intact if desired. Mix egg, mustard, spices together. Add shrimps mix and set aside. Mix cornmeal and flour in a plastic bag, shake well. Place shrimps in the cornflour shake well to coat. Put oil into a large frying pan on medium-high heat. Space shrimps while cooking do not overcrowd the pan. Let fry (2-3 minutes) on each side. Place on paper towels to let drain. Drizzle on your choice of sauce. Garnish with lemon wedges and parsley.

Yield: 8-10 serves

NEW ORLEANS FRIED OYSTERS

*Fried oysters make a great Po-Boy Sandwich.
Try make the very popular version the half and half Po-Boy the famous shrimp and oyster.
Try adding to a seafood platter. Any.........*

2 jar oysters (raw)

2 eggs (beaten)

1/8 oregano

Cayenne pepper (punch)

1/2 tsp black pepper

1/2 tsp salt

1/2 tsp french mustard

1 cup yellow cornmeal

1/3 cup flour (all-purpose)

2 cups vegetable oil

Remove oysters for their juice and drain. Place oil in frying pan and heat on medium-high heat. Combine cornmeal, flour, all spices shake well. Beat eggs and mustard together in a bowl. Next, add seasoned oysters to the mix. Roll oysters in cornflour and shake off excess cornflour. Let fry (2-3 minutes) on both sides. Remove pan and let drain. They are always served hot. Fried oysters make a great Po-Boy Sandwich.

CREOLE CRAWFISH ETOUFFEE

New Orleans here I come! Crawfish Etouffee flows in the blood of New Orleans people. I must attempt to the fact I did not grow up eating this dish. In my later years, I was introduced to it and I loved it, loved it, love it. This dish is another one of New Orleans's favorites. It can be enjoyed in most restaurants throughout the city. I craved the rich savory sauce with just a blast of cayenne. I also enjoyed the Crawfish Etouffee sister's dish, Shrimp Etouffee. Now that I am grown, I coin toss hoping it lands on the crawfish. Either one, it is an experience worth waiting to eat!

2-12 oz package crawfish (cleaned)

2-3 creole tomatoes (chopped fine)

1 yellow onion (chopped fine)

3 stalk green onions (chopped fine)

2 stalk celery (chopped fine)

1/2 green bell pepper (chopped fine)

3 cloves garlic (minced)

3 sprig parsley (mince)

2 bay leaves

1/2 tsp oregano

1/2 tsp basil

1/2 tsp thyme

1 tsp rosemary

1/2 tsp paprika

1 tsp cayenne pepper

1/4 tsp black pepper

1 tsp salt

1 stick butter

1/3 cup flour (all-purpose)

2 cups water

Make a light-colored roux using half a stick of butter and flour. Set aside. Place the other half of butter in a medium saucepan on low medium heat. Add onions, celery, and bell pepper to the pan. Saute until translucent (10 minutes). Add all spices, green onion, garlic, and parsley. Continue to saute (5 minutes). Add the crawfish tails, tomatoes, and bay leaves. Saute until the tails let off some of their liquid (5-7 minutes). Add roux. to the pan. Add water to your pan. Bring to a boil, then reduce to a simmer. Let cook (20-30 minutes). Your dish should have the consistency of a gravy, not too thick, not too thin. Taste test and adjust the spices and salt to taste. Remember etouffee is a hot and spicy dish. Don't be afraid of the spices. Remove the bay leaves and serve over steamed rice. Garnish with green onions, parsley, and a lemon wedge.

Yield: 4-6 serves

NEW ORLEANS JAMABALAYA

Everyone loves Creole Jambalaya. This dish can be found at every fair and festival through Southern Louisana. It is known and love for its spicy hot combinations of meats, sausages, chicken, shrimp, and rice. At the festivals, this is what I always order. Truly a mouth-watering dish sure to please the pallet. Creole Jambalaya is made with a basic brown gravy. You can try it Cajun and make it with the red gravy. The picture in this recipe shows the basic jambalaya blend. All you do is add your brown gravy roux or your red gravy with roux and you are all set to go.

Either way Bon Appetit!

2 pound raw shrimp (peeled and deveined)

1 pound ham or smoked sausage or both.

(cut ham into cubes-sausage into in slices)

1/2 pound chicken (cut into cube pieces)

2 lg yellow onion (chopped)

4 stalk green onion (chopped)

1/2 green bell pepper (chopped)

2 stalk celery (chopped)

3 cloves garlic (minced)

4 sprigs parsley

1 tsp basil

1 tsp oregano

1/2 tsp thyme

1 tsp rosemary

1 tsp paprika

2 bay leaves

1/2 tsp cayenne

1/2 tsp black pepper

1/4 tsp salt

1/2 cup butter

1/4 cup vegetable oil

1/4 cup flour (all-purpose)

2 cups water

Prepare all meats and seasonings. Add flour and oil to a small saucepan on medium heat. Make a roux and set aside. Place butter in a large pot on medium heat. Add chicken to the pot. Let cook, stirring often until chicken is light brown (15 minutes) Add ham and sausage to pot. Add all spices, onion, celery, bell pepper, and green onion to the pot. Allow to cook (20 minutes) or until soft. Add garlic to your pot. Add water and bring to a boil. Reduce heat to medium-low and add shrimps. Cover pot and simmer (15 minutes.) Taste test and add 2 cups of cooked rice. More rice may be added (your choice). Mix all together and taste test. This dish is a hot and very spicy one. Taste test again and adjust spices. Remove bay leaf before serving. You are good to go.

Yield: 10-12 servings

NEW ORLEANS FRIED SOFT SHELL CRAB

In the sixth and the seven ward the mom and pop restaurants were the place to go for this little treat. The grandmas and their sisters did the cooking in the restaurants, delicious. When I am in my home town, this is one of the treats I am looking up. Some of the restaurants call these little goodies, "Whales". Maybe it is because it has a whale of a flavor. From the juice crab taste to the seasoned just right crips crust, it will keep you coming back for more. The ones in this picture had a thick batter apply to them. Your choice of the extra thick batter or the regular thin batter these little whales are sure to please. I guarantee it. I always add these babies to my seafood platter and my family loves me for it. It was and still is a tradition for Good Friday "all you can eat seafood platter".

4-6 soft-shell crabs (cleaned)

2 eggs (beaten)

1/2 cup milk (buttermilk)

1 cup flour (all-purpose)

4-6 lemon wedges

1/2 tsp cayenne pepper

1/4 tsp black pepper

1/2 salt (to taste)

1/8 tsp thyme

1/4 tsp oregano

1/8 tsp sage

3 cups vegetable oil (for frying)

Clean and pat dry crabs. Heat oil in a Dutch oven on medium heat. Combine all spices and use half to season your crabs. Mix the other half of your spices, eggs, 1 cup flour, and milk to a pancake consistency or thicker. First, dredge crabs in the flour shaking off any excess. Then dip crabs into the batter. Dipping one crab at a time completely coating the crabs. Let any excess drip off. Carefully place the crabs into the oil upside down (this will make the claws stand up a bit for presentation). Fry two crabs at a time until they are golden brown on both sides, and they are floating to the top. Drain on paper towels. CAUTION, soft-shells have a tendency to squirt hot oil, or pop when the inside liquids heat up, so be very careful. Serve your crabs with your choice sauce. Garnishes of lemon wedge, sprinkles of minced garlic, and parsley.

Yield: 4-6 serving

CREOLE CRAB CAKES

Yield:

Daddy where you at!!! Daddy made them his way mama made them her way, needless to say,
it was all good. One way would be deep-fried crisp and the other way would be oven-fried.
Crab, the right seasoning, and your fingers of love, you are good to go. Delicious!

16 ozs crabmeat	**1**	Melt butter in a medium saucepan on medium heat.
1 stalk celery (finely chopped)	**2**	Add onions, celery, bell pepper to the pan.
1 small yellow onion (finely chopped)	**3**	Add green onions and garlic and saute until tender.
1/4 green bell pepper (finely chopped)		
1 stalk green onion (finely chopped)	**4**	Add crab meat, parsley, and spices to the pan.
2 cloves garlic (minced)	**5**	Stir and let cook (10 minutes) and set aside.
2 sprigs parsley (finely chopped)		
1-2 cups bread crumbs (plain)	**6**	In a mixing bowl add beaten eggs, bread crumbs, and all ingredients.
1/4 cup butter		
2-3 eggs (beaten)	**7**	Mix well, may add a little cream to make like a meatball.
1/4 tsp rosemary	**8**	Taste test just a little of the mix.
1/4 tsp oregano	**9**	Adjust salt and spices accordingly.
1/4 tsp cayenne pepper	**10**	Roll crab cake into balls and dust with flour.
1/4 tsp black pepper		
1/2 salt	**11**	Shape your crab cakes into mini like hamburgers.
1 cup flour (all-purpose)		
1-2 cup vegetable oil	**12**	Let fry oil on low medium heat until golden brown.
	13	Serve with your favorite seafood sauce.
	14	Garnish with lemon slices and parsley.

CREOLE STYLE SHRIMP STEW

Here is another one, just like the other ones. Yes, very delicious and power-packed with goodness. All you shrimp lovers know what I mean. Hot, savvy, and mama would have hers loaded with shrimp. The Creole-style Shimp Stew is prepared in brown gravy. I have always eaten it this way as a child. Now went mama would make this dish with red gravy, it is called Shrimp Creole or Shrimp Etouffee. Either way, you can not go wrong. I grew up eating this one and Shrimp Stew is still a part of my weekly menu. An oldie but a goodie. And I say to you Bon Appetit!

1-2 pounds raw shrimps (peeled and deveined)

1 large yellow onion (chopped)

3 stalk green onions (chopped)

1 stalks celery (chopped)

1/2 green bell pepper (chopped)

3 clove garlic (minced)

3 sprigs fresh parsley (minced)

1 bay leaf

1/2 teaspoon dried thyme

1/4 tsp oregano

1/2 tsp rosemary

1/4 tsp paprika

1/4 tsp black pepper

1/4 tsp cayenne pepper

1/2 tsp salt

1/4 cup flour (all-purpose)

1/2 cup butter

2-3 cups water

*When using 1 pound of shrimps cut the ingredients in half. Place 1/4 cup butter and flour in a small saucepan. Make a roux (medium-light brown) on medium heat and set aside. In a large saucepan on medium heat add a 1/4 cup of butter. Add the onions, celery, and bell pepper to the pan. Cook stirring from time to time until tender (5-7 minutes). Add garlic, green onions, and parsley to the pan. Allow to cook (5 minutes). Add all spices, roux, and two cups of water. Bring to a boil. Continue to cook for (15-20 minutes). Stir in the shrimp and allow to cook (15-20 minutes) on low heat. Add more water a little at a time (if needed). Taste test and add spices and salt accordingly. This is a very spicy dish, so don't be afraid of the spices. Serve over steamed rice. Can boil your shrimp shells and use that water in your dish. Served with steamed rice. Garnish with parsley/paprika/cayenne and enjoy. Try some thinly sliced toasted french bread on the side. One of New Orlean's oldest dishes.

Yield: 4 serves

CREOLE STYLE BEEF TONGUE

Creole-style Beef Tongue is truly another sixth ward creole dish. You will hear me say this quite offend in my book because these dishes were the everyday meals of the people of New Orleans. As a child, I can still remember my mother cooking this dish for the family. Sometimes she would prepare it on top of the stove and then sometimes she would prepare it in the oven. I enjoyed both ways. This dish calls for a dark brown roux. Dishes such as beef stew, oxtail, beef roast, game meat, always make your roux a dark brown. Pork dishes, gumbos, smothered dishes, etc. calls for a medium brown roux are lighter. Creole-style Beef Tongue always made a very satisfying and tasty Sunday dinner. Served with steamed rice and some of your favorite side dishes, you are in for a treat in flavor and satisfaction.

1 3-4 pound beef tongue	1/8 tsp sage
1 large yellow onion (chopped)	1/2 tsp black pepper
3 fresh green onions (chopped)	1 tsp salt
1/4 green bell pepper (chopped)	1/4 cup flour
4 cloves garlic (chopped)	2 cups water
4 sprigs fresh parsley (chopped)	1/4 cup vegetable oil
2 bay leaves	1/8 cup butter
1/4 tsp oregano	1 tablespoon salt*
1/2 tsp rosemary	2 cups water to cover the tongue
1/4 tsp thyme	

Wash the meat in a large heavy-based pot. Put in a large pot of water to submerge the tongue. Bring to the boil then leave to cook on medium heat (10-15 minutes). Drain and set aside. When cool peel off the outer skin. Add butter to a dutch oven on medium heat. Add tongue to pot and brown all sides. Remove from pot and set aside. When cool enough to slice, slice into 1/2 inch pieces. Set slices aside. Add oil and flour to make a roux. Drop onions and bell pepper in the pot. Let cook (5 minutes) on low. Next, add sliced tongue to the pot. Stir then add garlic, parsley, and all spices to the pot. Add water to the pot and bring to a boil on medium-high heat. Cover the pot and let cook on low to low-medium until meat is tender (1-2 hours). It is ready when meat can be easily pierced through with a fork. Taste test and adjust spices and salt. Let cook until you get to the gravy consistency you desire. This dish is served with steamed rice and your choice of salad and vegetables. This is truly a New Orleans Creole dish. Bon Appetit!

Yield: 6-8 serving

STEWED EGGS IN TOMATO GRAVY

This dish is a much eaten Lenten dish. Remember the New Orleans creoles old were Catholics. Especially the sixth and the seven wards. Yes, my mothers, their mothers, and grandmothers would cook this meal during the Lenten seasons. It was cooked with a rich red gravy, no roux, and hard boil eggs over spaghetti. So easy to make yet so good and I loved it. I would make this dish for my children and I would tell them about the days of old. Old New Orleans, Old sixth ward, and the old-style dishes that they served at the dinner tables each day.

12 eggs (hard-boiled)

2-3 cans tomato sauce

1 can crushed tomatoes

1 yellow onion (chopped)

1/4 green bell pepper (chopped)

4 stalk green onions (chopped)

3 cloves garlic (minced)

3 sprigs fresh parsley (minced)

2 bay leaves

1/4 tsp basil

1 tsp rosemary

1/2 tsp paprika

1/4 tsp oregano

1/8 tsp black pepper

cayenne pepper (pinch)

1/2 tsp salt

1 tbsp sugar

2-3 cans water

1 can water from crushed tomatoes

4 tbsp butter or 1/4 cup vegetable oil

1/4 cup flour (all-purpose)

Fit a large pot with water and bring to a boil. Place eggs in and let hard-boil (10 minutes). In a large saucepan put butter over medium heat. Add all seasonings and saute (5-7 minutes). Add garlic and saute (1-2 minutes) more. Add all spices and cook (2 minutes) more. Add tomato sauce and cook for (5-7 minutes). Next, add crushed tomatoes and water to the pan. Mix flour and oil/butter in a small saucepan on medium heat. Make a light brown roux and add to the pot. Bring to a boil. Toss in bay leaves and allow the mixture to cook (60 minutes) on low-medium heat. Let cook uncovered, stirring occasionally. Drop in the eggs and cook (30 minutes) more. Check your water lever. More add may be added to the dish if needed. Taste test for spices and salt. Remove bay leaves. Served over spaghetti. This is truly one of New Orleans' Lenten dishes.

Yield: 6 serves

PINAY VEAL CHOPS

When I was a little girl growing up in the sixth ward of New Orleans, my mother would make her Pinay' Chops with veal round chops. You remember the ones with the little round bone in the middle. She would serve them with creamy mashed potatoes, veggies, and a nice salad. Yes, I can still remember it one because Pinay' Veal Chop was one of my favorites. Well, I think all of them were my favorites because my mama was a very good cook. I want to say, hat off all to all of the mothers and grandmothers of my old neighborhood. And to all of the good cooks of New Orleans. You helped in making us what we are today. We were a village. And I have to say our fathers stood strong.

4 veal chops (your choice)

3 eggs

garlic powder (pinch)

basil (pinch)

1/2 tsp rosemary

1/8 tsp oregano

1/8 tsp paprika

1/8 tsp black pepper

1/2 tsp salt

2 cups breadcrumbs (plain)

3/4 cup butter

2 cups vegetable oil

Wash veal chops. Pat the veal chops so they are as dry as possible. Season and dust with flour. In a shallow bowl, crack eggs and beat. In another bowl, place the breadcrumbs. Dip the chops in the beaten egg. Let any excess egg drip off before placing it in the breadcrumbs. Coat chops entirely. Pat down the breadcrumbs well. Rest in the refrigerator (30 minutes). Place butter in a large frying pan on low-medium heat. Place chops in your frying pan. Turn the chops once and continue frying until cooked through (8-10 minutes) per side. You may need to cook just two chops at a time. If so use half the butter for each pair of chops. Remove from the pan and place on a wire rack with paper towels. Place uncovered somewhere to keep warm. Serve warm with your choice of sides. Garnish with parsley and enjoy.

Yield: 4 serves

STUFFED MIRLITON

OMG, how this dish brings back memories of my childhood. My daddy had a mirliton vine in our back yard. At Thanksgiving and Christmas time, daddy would have enough to give all of his neighbors and family. My brother Charlie and I called ourselves the mirliton brigade because we took care of the vine and its trellis. Remember my daddy was a Merchant Marine and when daddy was away working we were happy to man his ship. A mirliton vine was of the norm in the sixth and seventh wards. Along with figs, pears, and persimmons trees were very common in all the neighbors of New Orleans. I enjoyed this dish as a little girl and I still enjoy eating mirlitons each and every holiday.

6 mirlitons

1 pound shrimp peeled, deveined(chopped)

1/2 lb ham (chopped)

2 yellow onion (chopped)

4 stalk green onions (chopped)

1/2 bell pepper (chopped)

4 sprigs fresh parsley (minced)

3 cloves garlic (minced)

1/2 tsp thyme

1/2 tsp rosemary

1/2 tsp oregano

2 bay leaves

1/2 tsp cayenne

1/8 tsp black pepper

1 tsp salt

1/2 cup butter

1 cup water

2-3 cups bread crumbs (plain)

Preheat the oven to 350. Cut mirliton in half and place in a large saucepan. Cover with water, bring to a boil, and cook (15-25 minutes). Remove mirliton from the water and allow them to cool. When cool enough to handle, remove the pit and scoop out all its meat. Reserve the shells and set the meat aside. In a saucepan over medium heat put in butter, onions, bell pepper, and green onions saute (10-12 minutes). Add garlic, green onions, parsley, and ham cook (5-10 minutes). Next, add mirliton, all spices, and bay leaves to the pot. Add the shrimps and cook on low (30 minutes). Stir occasionally to prevent sticking. Add bread crumbs and water to the pot. Can add more water and bread crumbs. Taste test and adjust spices and salt. Allow simmering (15 minutes). Taste test once more. Then stuff the mirliton halves. Next, sprinkle the remaining bread crumbs on top of your mirlitons. Bake until toasty brown (15-20 minutes). And have it your way with one of your favorite sides.

Yield: 12 serving

SIXTH WARD BEEF STEW

Sixth Ward Beef Stew was another one of my favorite. I guess you are saying here she goes again. But I really mean it this time. My favorite choice of meat for this dish was short ribs. I love the flat bones on the ribs too me, it made the dish taste all the better. My mother did not cook her stew with carrots. She just used Irish potatoes in a well seasoned brown gravy. It was served over steamed rice. As a child, I would put ketchup on my stew and I still put Ketchup on my beef stew when I cook it. My big cousins Charles and Wallace "Peter" would put ketch on their stew too. I remember that so many years ago. Big cousin is a term used in New Orleans that meant older cousins.

2 -3 pounds beef chuck (cubed), short ribs, or stew meat

2 Irish potatoes (peeled and cubed)

1 large yellow onion (chopped)

1/2 bell pepper (chopped)

4 stalk green onions (chopped)

3 cloves garlic (chopped)

4 sprigs fresh parsley (minced)

2 bay leaves

1/8 tsp sage

1/8 tsp thyme

1/4 tsp oregano

1/2 tsp rosemary

1/4 tsp paprika

1 tsp salt

1/2 tsp black pepper

4 tbsp butter

1/2 cup flour

5-6 cups water

Wash meat and pat dry. Season with spices in a large bowl. Next, dust meat with flour and mix. Heat butter in a large Dutch oven over medium-low heat. Add meat and cook until meat has browned. Add the onions and bell pepper. Stir and allow to cook (7-10 minutes) You may have to pour a very small amount of water in the pot to prevent burning or sticking. Add garlic, green onions, parsley, water, and bring to a boil (5-7) Reduce heat, cover, and simmer. Mix flour and oil in a small saucepan to make a roux. Add slowly to the stew stirring constantly. Simmer covered (5-10). Add the potatoes to the stew. Cover and cook another (30 minutes) Or until potatoes are tender. Taste test and adjust spices and salt accordingly. Serve over steamed rice and a salad of your choice.

Yield: 6-8 serves

SMOTHERED PORK CHOPS

This dish still stands in my eyesight. Good and tasty as a child and go and tasty for me as an adult. Breakfast or dinner it will hit the stop. Mana served her smother pork chop over steamed rice. When she would fry her chops she served them want mashed potatoes. Back in the days, you could find this dish on the mama's and pop's restaurant in the breakfast section. There was nothing like smothered pork chop from a mama's and pop's. Finger-licking, good.

4-6 large pork chops (your choice)

2 large yellow onions (halved and thinly sliced)

2 clove garlic (minced)

2 sprigs parsley Minced)

1 tsp rosemary

1/2 tsp oregano

1/2 tsp black pepper

1 tsp salt

3/4 cup all-purpose flour

4 tbsp butter

1/4 cup vegetable oil

1- cup water

Rinse and pat dry chops. Dust chops with flour. Place chops in a large bowl and season using all of your spices. In a large saucepan on medium-low heat put in your oil or your butter. Add chops cook until both sides are browned (5-6 minutes) on each side. Let cook (3 minutes) more. Transfer the chop to a plate and set aside. Add onions to your pan. Saute' until onions are tender (5-7 minutes). Add garlic to the pot. Reduce heat to low and let cook stirring (2-3 Minutes). Add water in slowly stirring until mix. Reduce heat to simmer and add chops and any juice from the plate. Add parsley and taste test. May add more spices and salt. Let simmer until cooked until tender (20-25 minutes) covered. Remember Smothered Chops comes with a short gravy this not a stew. Serve over steamed rice.

Yield: 4-6 servings

OVEN BAKED RABBIT STEW

When I was entering this recipe, I could not help but think of my Uncle Hunter and my Auntie Pill. My Uncle Hunter was known and loved for his hunting abilities. My Auntie Pill was known for her good cooking and the love she showed to us. Love you, Auntie Pill and Uncle Hunter for this is what the family called them (their creole nicknames). I remember the wild game (rabbits, ducks, quail, and pheasant) you would send to my mother. Auntie Alice would bring rabbits and ducks to mama on her trips to the city. Rabbit stew is a much sort after dish in the restaurants of New Orleans. As a child, I enjoy this dish and I now cook it for my friends for them to enjoy.

1 rabbit (cleaned and cut up)

2 slices bacon (cut in pieces)

2 yellow onions (chopped)

2 stalk green onions (chopped)

1/4 green bell pepper (chopped)

3 cloves garlic (minced)

1 stalk celery (chopped)

2 sprigs fresh parsley (minced)

1/8 tsp oregano

1/8 tsp thyme

1/4 tsp paprika

1/4 tsp rosemary

2 bay leaves

1/8 tsp Black pepper

1 tsp salt

cayenne pepper (pinch)

3 tbsp flour (all-purpose)

3 tbsp butter

2 tbsp olive oil

2 cups water

Wash rabbit and pat dry. Preheat oven to 225 degrees. Add garlic and 1 cup water to the rabbit. Marinade all the rabbit pieces with the mixture and let rest (30 minutes) to absorb all the flavors. Mix butter and flour in a small saucepan to make a roux and set aside. After 30 minutes have passed, place your rabbit in a baking pan and place in the oven. Add roux and the remaining 1 cup of water. Add all seasoning and spices. Allow baking for (40-50 minutes)turning over from time to time. Loosely tent with foil. Baste and continue baking (15-20 minutes). Be careful not to let your rabbit dry out or burn. You may add water if needed. Taste test and adjust spices. This is truly another New Orleans Creole dish. This dish is served over steamed rice.

Yield: 4-6 serves

SMOTHERED LIVER

Smothered Liver you either love it or you hate it, there is no in-between. As a little girl, I have always loved the dish. And to me, the more onions the better it tasted. My mama cooked her liver with plenty of onions and steamed rice and her side was creamed style corn. On the menus of restaurants in New Orleans, this dish makes a great breakfast. For breakfast serve it with grits and your style of eggs.

Always serve smothered liver hot and over steamed rice. I love, love, love this dish!

1-2 pounds liver (veal)

2-3 large yellow onions (sliced)

2 clove garlic (minced)

1/2 tsp oregano

1 tsp rosemary

1 tsp paprika

1/4 tsp black pepper

cayenne pepper (pinch)

1/2 tsp salt, to taste

1/4 cup butter

1/2 cup flour (all-purpose) enough to coat liver

1/2 cup water

Heat butter on medium-low heat in a large saucepan. Season liver with the spices. Coat both sides of the liver with flour. When the oil is heated, brown liver on both sides (5 minutes) per side. Add onions and saute until tender. Remove onion mixture and set aside. Combine water and garlic to pan stir and let it come to boil. If the mixture becomes too thick, add more water to the pan. Add liver back to pan, put onion mixture on top of your liver. Simmer for 20-25 minutes. Our Smother Liver is served with steam rice and cream style corm on the side.

Yield: 5-6 serves

CREOLE STYLE MEATLOAF

This dish made a great and delicious Sunday meal. Loaded with goodness, rich in spices, and seasoned to the brim a meatloaf dinner truly would hit the spot. Mama served baked macaroni with hers. A nice crisp salad and did I tell you creoles love peas. Yes, we do. Nice creamy pea with lots of butter. Can be served with your choice of pasta, steamed rice, or mashed potatoes.

2-3 pounds lean ground beef

2-3 eggs

1-2 cup bread crumbs (plain)

2-3 15 ounces can tomato sauce

2 yellow onions (chopped fine)

4 green onions (chopped fine)

1/2 green bell pepper (chopped fine)

2 stalk celery (chopped fine)

3 cloves of garlic (minced)

4 sprigs parsley (minced)

2 bay leaves

1/4 tsp each oregano and sage

1/4 tsp thyme and basil

1/1 tsp paprika and rosemary

1/4 tsp black pepper

cayenne (pinch)

1 tsp salt

Additional flour, for coating

4 tbsp flour (all-purpose) for the roux

2-15 ounce can of water

1/2 cup milk (evaporated)

1/4 cup vegetable oil

2 tbsp butter

Preheat the oven to 350 degrees. Place the ground beef in a large bowl and set aside. Heat the butter over medium heat. Add the onions, bell pepper, and celery until tender. Add garlic, green onions, and parsley cook (3 minutes). Transfer to a plate and set aside. Add oil and flour on medium-high heat in a saucepan. Made roux medium brown then set aside. Slowly mix in tomato sauce, half of the spices, bay leaves, and water then return to heat. Bring to a boil, reduce heat, and simmer (15 minutes). Creole taste test and adjust accordingly. Blend together milk and eggs. Add bread crumbs, the other half of the seasonings, the other half of the spices, the milk and egg mix, to the ground beef. Blend everything together. Mix gently and shape into a loaf. The mixture should be firm. If it is breaking apart, return to the bowl and additional bread crumbs until it holds together. Place your meatloaf in a large baking pan. Dust with flour and put in the oven. Allow meatloaf to brown. Once browned, pour the gravy over it. Let bake (60 minutes) bast a few times while baking. Allow cooking until done. Remove from the oven and garnish with parsley. Serve with steamed rice or pasta and your favorite sides.

Yield: 6 to 8 servings

SMOTHERED CHICKEN

When I start thinking about home and the foods we used to eat and the flavors, I start pulling out the pots. And as we used to say in the sixth ward, "it is on". Smothered chicken back in the days was cooked using a whole chicken cut up in pieces. And when I start thinking about smothered chicken and the way mama cooked it, I want it just the way my mama used to cook it. Think about it and be honest went you start reminiscing about the foods and the way it used to be. We all start pulling on the pots or we try to find someone that knows what they are doing. Smothered chicken was made with springer and when your mamas and your grandmothers made stewed chicken they would use hen. Believe me, you can taste the difference. Back in the days the way it was. This meal is served over rice. I eat this all the time. Quick, easy, and good!

3-3 1/2 pounds chicken (cut up)

1 yellow onion (chopped)

3 green onions (chopped)

1/4 green bell pepper (chopped)

2 cloves garlic (minced)

2 sprigs fresh parsley (chopped)

1 tsp rosemary

1/4 oregano

1/4 tsp black pepper

1 tsp salt

3/4 cup flour (all-purpose)

4 tbsp butter

2 cups water

Clean and rinse chicken. Place chicken in a bowl season using all of the spices. Next, thoroughly coat the chicken with the flour. Heat butter in a Dutch oven over medium-high heat. Brown the chicken in 2 batches, cooking (4-5 minutes) on each side. Place chicken on a plate and set aside. Reduce the heat to medium-low. Add the onions and bell pepper to the pot and cook (5 minutes) stirring occasionally to prevent sticking. Add the green onions, garlic, and parsley to your pot (2-3 minutes). Next, add water to the pot and stir cook (3-4 minutes) Add the chicken, bay leaves, and bring to a simmer. May add a half cup to a cup more water if you should need it. Remember Creole Smothered Chicken has a short gravy not a long gravy like a stew. Simmer gently for 30 minutes or until the chicken is tender. Taste test and then adjust accordingly. This dish is served with steamed rice and any of your favorite sides.

Yield: 6 servings

MEATBALLS & SPAGHETTI

Now tell me, who doesn't like Meatball and spaghetti? A great meal for a child. I am saying this because all of my family and friends loved it. From the rich zesty gravy to the big juice meatball it was just what a hungry belly needed and more. I use to call it the double hitter because of the double seasoned gravy and meatball. Bring in the creole seasoned garlic bread, a nice crisp green salad, and you are all set. Don't forget to garnish your dish with your choice of grated cheese. It's a winner!

2 pounds ground beef

1-15 ounce can tomato sauce

1-15 ounce can whole tomatoes

1 cup bread crumbs (plain)

2 eggs

12 yellow onion (chopped)

3 stalk green onions (chopped)

1/2 green bell pepper (chopped)

3 cloves garlic (chopped)

3 sprigs fresh parsley (minced)

2 tbsp basil (finely chopped)

1/4 tsp oregano

1/4 tsp sage

1 tsp rosemary

1/4 tsp thyme

1/4 tsp black pepper

1/8 tsp cayenne

1 tsp salt

1 tbsp sugar

2 Tbsp vegetable oil

1 cup flour (all-purpose)

1 cup vegetable oil

2-15 ounce can water

1 pound spaghetti

Heat oil in 4-5 quart pot on medium heat. Add onions, bell pepper, green onions and cook (3-5 minutes). Add garlic and cook (1-2 minutes). Take out half of the seasoning from the pot and put aside. Add sugar, tomato sauce and chopped tomatoes. Add half of the spices and bay leaf to the pot. Reduce heat and simmer while preparing meatballs. Stirring occasionally to keep from sticking. Mix by hand in a large bowl the beef, eggs, milk, the other half of spices, breadcrumbs, and the other half of the seasoning. Do not over-mix or the meatballs will be tough. Form 2 inch round meatballs. Roll and compress into tight balls. Heat frying pan on medium-high heat. Add oil to the frying pan. Dust meatballs in flour and add to the pan. Brown meatballs on all sides 3-4 minutes. Brown meatballs all around. Cook in a single layer and do not over-cook. Add meatballs and 2 cans of water to sauce & simmer. Taste test sauce and adjust spices and salt. Simmer sauce and meatballs (30-45 minutes). Stirring occasionally. Taste test again. Serve meatball over spaghetti or pasta of choice. Prepare pasta according to the direction on package.

SMOTHERED CABBAGE

Yes, now we are talking Smothered Cabbage. This my most favorite dish. It comes before gumbo, red beans, smothered anything, and seafood. From a little girl, I just loved it. Mama would cook her cabbage with pickled pigtails, pickled tips, and ham. She would always bake a large pan of buttery cornbread to go along with it. I would be in seven heavens. As a little girl, I could always enjoy a good plate of cabbage, and please do not forget the cornbread.

1-2 cabbages(cleaned and cut)

2 ham hock,

1 pound pickled meat

1 pound pickled pigtails

2 yellow onion (chopped)

3 stark green onions (chopped)

1 stalk celery (chopped)

1/4 green bell pepper (chopped)

2 cloves garlic (minced)

1 bay leaf

1/8 tsp oregano

1/8 tsp thyme

1/2 tsp paprika

1/8 tsp sage

1 tsp rosemary

1/8 tsp black pepper

cayenne (pinch)

1/2 tsp salt (add salt at the very end of cooking)

1/3 cup flour

1/4 cup butter

1 cups of water

Wash and clean your cabbage and set aside. Prepare and wash all meats. Place all meat in a large pot and add water to cover the meat 3 inches above the meat. Cook until your meat on medium heat until tender and put aside. Do not toss the water. When cool enough to handle cut meat into desired slices and put aside. Add butter to another large pot and hon medium heat. Add yellows, celery, and bell pepper to the pot. Saute (10 minutes). Add green onions and garlic to the pot let cook (5 minutes. Stir and let cook (5-7 minutes). Start with the water from the meat and pour 1 cup into the pot. Add all spices and bay leaves to the pot. Mix flour and water to the consistency of gravy and add to your pot. Add cabbage to the pot. Cook cabbage over medium to low heat (40 minutes) or until your cabbage gets to your tender preference. Taste test after (30 minutes) and adjust spices accordingly. Then taste test for spices again at the end. Creole cabbage is served with steamed rice and a piece of buttery cornbread on the side.

Yield: 6-8 serves

CREOLE SMOTHERED VEAL CHOPS

Does anyone remember the seven chop? Seven chops also were called the gravy chops back in the days. This dish would be served during the week. some other cuts of meat used as gravy chops were chuck and rounds but the most popular was the seven. Remember with the little seven shape bone. Creole-style smothered veal/beef chops are made with a short gravy. It is not a stew, stewed dish has a longer gravy. No roux because the dusting of your chops will form the roux. This dish is well seasoned and flavorful because it is served with steamed rice. With a nice scoop of potato salad or a fresh salad, this dish is sure to please. Your choice of veggies and your family will love you for it.

6 - 7 veal chops (or your choice)

1 yellow onion (chopped)

3 stalks green onions (chopped)

1/2 green bell pepper (chopped)

2 cloves garlic (minced)

3 sprigs fresh parsley

1/4 cup butter or vegetable oil

1/4 tsp oregano

1/8 tsp thyme

1/2 tsp rosemary

1/2 tsp black pepper

1/2 tsp salt

1/2 cup flour (all-purpose)

1-2 cups water

Rinse chops, pat dry, and all spices and place aside. In a large saucepan or dutch oven heat butter/oil on medium-high heat. Dust chops with flour and place into the pan. Can turn down the heat if needed. Brown chops on both sides then remove from the pan and set aside. Lower heat to low- medium. Add onions and bell pepper to pan, saute (6-7 minutes). Next add garlic, green onions, and parsley sauteing another (5 minutes). Add water and stir and bring to a boil. Taste test and adjust. Add chops to the pan and cover and cook on low heat (30 minutes). Stir from time to time to keep chops from sticking. If need to add water, add a 1/4 cup at a time. Taste test and adjust spice and salt if needed. Continue cooking (20-30 minutes) or until meat is tender. Serve with steamed rice and your favorite sides.

Yield: 6 to 8 serving

MUSTARD GREENS

The most popular greens for the surrounding area of New Orleans was mustard. And oh how I loved them as a child. Mama would cook them with pickled meat and smoked ham hock. Creole people are lovers of rice. Mama served her mustard greens with steamed rice. She also baked a buttery cornbread to go along with it. Some of the other greens, we loved and was cooked were turnip and spinach. We did not eat cornbread with every meal we were into our french bread and other kinds of bread with our meal. But I must say give me my cornbread with my greens and my cabbage. It is a must-have for me. I think I can safely say, "you can tell Louisiana folks by the amount of rice they eat". We are definitely rice eating people.

8-10 bunches mustard greens (cleaned and cut)

2 ham hock,

1 pound pickled meat

1 pound smoked neck bones

1 large yellow onion (chopped)

4 stark green onions (chopped)

1 stalk celery (chopped)

1/2 green bell pepper (chopped)

3 cloves garlic (minced)

1 bay leaf

1/4 tsp oregano

1/8 tsp thyme

1/2 tsp paprika

1/4 tsp sage

1 tsp rosemary

1/8 tsp black pepper

cayenne (pinch)

1/2 tsp salt (add salt at the very end of cooking)

1/3 cup flour

1/4 cup butter

6-8 cups of water

Wash and clean your greens and set aside. Prepare and wash all meats. Place all meat in a large pot and add water to cover the meat 4 inches above the meat. Cook until your meat is almost tender and put aside. Do not toss the water. When cool enough to handle cut meat into desired slices and place aside. In another large pot add butter and heat on medium heat. Add yellows, celery, and bell pepper to the pot. Saute (10 minutes). Add green onions and garlic to the pot let **cook (5 minutes. Stir and let cook (5-7 minutes).** Start with the water from the meat and pour 4 cups into the pot. Add all spices, bay leaves, and greens to the pot. Mix flour and water the consistency of gravy and add to your pot. Cook the greens over medium to low heat for 40 minutes or until they get to your tender preference. Taste test after (30 minutes) and adjust greens accordingly. Then taste test for spices again. Creole mustard greens are served with steamed rice and buttery cornbread.

Yield: 6-8 serving

STUFFED CRAB

Who many of us could not wait for Friday to get here? Why, because your mother stuffed crabs were on the menu? Hurry up Friday stuffed crabs is on the menu. As a child, I enjoyed the way my mother prepare her crabs. Filled with crab meat, all the seasoning, and overstuffed, it was yummy to my tummy. Remember Creole were Catholics back in the days. My book is about the foods and everyday menus of the 1950s and early 1960s. Its food, how it was prepared, and the seasoning and the spices our mothers used in their dishes. Fridays were seafood day. Needless to say, Friday was dobbed Friday Fish Fry Day. All most everyone in New Orleans and the surrounding areas eats some kind of seafood dishes on Fridays. So good and tasty. Why do New Orleans people love crabs? I think it's because of the freshness. Hi, sixth ward thanks for all of the Friday Fish Frys and the delicious stuffed crabs.

16 ounces crabmeat

8 crab shells

1/4 cup butter

1 yellow onion (finely chopped)

2 stalk green onions (finely chopped)

2 cloves garlic (minced)

2 cups bread crumbs (use 1/2 cup for topping)

2 sprigs fresh parsley (minced)

1/8 tsp oregano

1/8 1/8 thyme

1/2 tsp rosemary

1/8 tsp cayenne pepper

1/8 tsp black pepper

salt (to taste)

1 egg

Preheat oven to 350 degrees. In a large saucepan over medium heat, melt butter. Add the onions saute (3-5 minutes). Add green onions, garlic, and parsley saute another (3-5 minutes). Reduce heat to low heat and simmer until seasoning is tender. Next, fold in crabmeat. Add all spices to the pot. Add beaten eggs and bread crunches. Mix well and taste test. Adjust spices and salt accordingly. Remove from heat. Spoon crab mixture into crab shells. Sprinkle tops with bread crumbs. Bake until heated through and golden brown on top (15-20 minutes). Serve warm. May be served with your favorite seafood sauce. My favorite is the "Lobster Creme".

Yield: 4-8 servings

SMOTHERED SQUASH

True Creole-style cooking at its best. I do not know of anyone in New Orleans who doesn't like smothered squash. I remember my mother would cook it for my Auntie Alice. She enjoyed this dish so and would look forward to mama cooking this dish for her whenever she would come to town. In her famous words, "good eating Magelet, good eating". This dish is a loved and highly sort after one in New Orleans. What about a nice glass of homemade wine with this one? Show enough Creole eating, I guarantee!!! Bon Appetit!

1 pound raw shrimp (peeled and deveined)

1/2 pound ham (chopped into tiny pieces)

6-8 large yellow squash (diced)

2 yellow onions (chopped)

3 stalks green onions (chopped)

1/2 green bell pepper (chopped)

3 cloves garlic (minced)

3 sprigs parsley (minced)

2 bay leaves

1/2 tsp oregano

1/4 tsp thyme

1 tsp rosemary

1/4 tsp cayenne pepper

1/4 tsp black pepper

1/2 tsp salt

1/2 cup butter

1-2 cups water

Prepare squash wash, peel, and slice into small pieces. Put in a pot with water on high heat. Bring to a boil. Then let cook (20 minutes) Remove from heat and drain and set aside. In a large saucepan over medium-high heat put in the butter. Add onions and bell peppers saute (5-7 minutes). Add garlic, green onions, and parsley saute (4-6 minutes). Lower heat to low medium. Stirring frequently to prevent garlic from burning. Stir in ham cooking (5-10 minutes). Reduce heat to low, add shrimp cooking another (6-8 minutes). Next, add water, squash, and all spices cooking another (15 minutes). Stir to keep from sticking. Mix well. Before adding the squash to the pot chopped up as much as possible. Cover and let simmer on lower (20-25 minutes) or until ham is tender. Creole taste test can add more spices and salt if needed. Smothered squash is supposed to a have kick to it, so don't be afraid of the cayenne pepper. Smothered Squash has the consistency of stuffed mirlitons/stuffed bell peppers before the bread crumbs are added. It is always served over steamed rice. Do not forget your sliced french bread.

Yield: 6-8 servings

STUFFED EGGPLANT

This dish is Creole cooking for sure. As a little girl, I remembered how the family enjoyed this dish. Another one of my Auntie Alice's favorites. When cooked during the week it was a main dish, but when cooked on Sundays it became a side dish. For Sunday dinner it wold be served with roast, a fourth of eggplant as a side with rice and gravy and a choice of salad. As a child either with beef or poultry, it made a mighty fine Sunday dinner. My choice of salad would a tossed salad. I would be in seventh heaven. All of the little grannies were known for this one.

4 eggplants

1 pound ham (chopped)

1 pound Shrimp deveined (chopped)

2 eggs (beaten)

2 large yellow onion (chopped)

1/2 green bell pepper (chopped)

3 stalk green onions (chopped)

4 sprigs parsley (chopped)

3 clove garlic (minced)

1 bay leaf

1/4 tsp thyme

1/2 tsp oregano

1/2 tsp paprika

1/4 tsp basil

1/2 tsp rosemary

1/4 tsp cayenne pepper

1/4 tsp black pepper

1 tsp salt

1/2 cup butter

2 cups bread crumbs (plain)

1/2 cup milk (whole)

1-2 cup water

Preheat oven to 350-375 degrees. Next bring water to boil in a Dutch Oven. Bring to a boil and add sliced eggplants (cut down the middle, lengthwise). Let boil (20 minutes). Gently remove from pot and let drain. When cool enough to handle remove the eggplant meat from its shell and put it in a bowl. Chop and set aside. Chop ham and shrimps and set them aside. Melt the butter in a large saucepan on medium heat. Add the onions and bell pepper sauteing (7-10 minutes). Add green onions, garlic, parsley, and all spices to the pan cook (4-6 minutes). Add ham to the pan cook (5 minutes). Next add shrimps continue cooking (5 minutes). Add the eggplant to the pot. Stir to keep from sticking. Next, add water milk and egg beat mixture before adding to your pan. Let cook (15-20 minutes) on low heat. Stir as you pour the mixture into the pan. Add the bread crumbs a little at a time until the right consistency is achieved. Not too wet, not too dry. Taste test and adjust with spices and salt. This is a spicy dish so please add the spiced especially cayenne pepper. Put the eggplant mixture into its shells or put the filling into a baking pan and place in the oven. Sprinkle top with bread crumbs. Bake until slightly golden brown (30-40 minutes). Remove for oven and allow the sit (5-10 minutes). Enjoy! This dish aims to please.

Yield: 4-8 servings

SMOTHERED SNAP BEANS

Smothered snap beans were definitely on the weekday household menus. Back in the days, this dish was cooked with pickled meat or ham. Either way, it served as a great satisfying meal. As a little girl, it was one of my favorites and it still is today. Mothers and grandmothers cooked every day and they loved doing it. Good cooks, good people, and good food. Those were the days. New Orleans, sixth ward creole style. There was nothing better than a hot plate of smothered snap beans. Everyone loved and enjoy this dish. From its fresh green bean to its good and taste gravy it was definitely a treat at anyone's dinner. Mama cooked snap beans and she served it over rice. When I cook snap bean I serve it over rice too. It's a New Orleans thing. We love rice can't you tell?

2-3 pounds green beans
(trimmed, halved, or leave whole)

1/2 pound Salt pork

1 pound ham (cut into small pieces)

2-3 Irish potatoes (diced)

2 yellow onions (chopped)

2 stalks green onions (chopped)

1/4 bell pepper (chopped)

2 cloves garlic (minced)

3 sprigs fresh parsley (minced)

1/4 tsp oregano

1/2 tsp rosemary

1/8 black pepper

1/2 tsp salt

cayenne (pinch)

3 tbsp butter

2 cups water

1 tsp flour (all-purpose)

Put all meat in a pot add water to cover the meat about 2 inches above meat. Bring the pot to a boil on medium-high and let cook until meat is almost tender. Place meat aside do not toss water. In a saucepan on medium heat add the butter to the pan. Add the onions and bell pepper saute (4 minutes). Lower heat to medium-low. Add green onions and garlic to your pot stir (5 minutes). Next, add all meat and flour to the pot. Next, add all spices and green beans and stir Add 2 cups of water(use the water from out of the meat pot) to your beans. Bring to a boil, reduce the heat, and simmer and cook (60 minutes). After cooking for 30 minutes add potatoes to the pot. Stir from time to time to keep from sticking. Taste test May use more water as much as need. No salt was added to this recipe due to the salt content that is already in the meat. You can always add your salt at the end of the taste test. Now taste test. This dish can be eaten two way more potatoes eaten by itself. Or you can have fewer potatoes and serve it on steamed rice.

Yield: 6+ servings

NEW ORLEANS SIDE DISHES

In this section are the many dishes used as everyday side dishes. These Creole sode dishes went quite will with beef, veal, pork, poultry, game and seafood.

STUFFED EGGPLANT

This dish is Creole cooking for sure. As a little girl, I remembered how the family enjoyed this dish. Another one of my Auntie Alice's favorites. When cooked during the week it was the main dish, but when cooked on Sundays it became a side dish. For Sunday dinner it would be served with roast, a fourth of eggplant as a side with rice and gravy and a choice of salad. As a child either with beef or poultry, it made a mighty fine Sunday dinner. My choice of salad would a tossed salad. I would be in seventh heaven. All of the little grannies were known for this one. Remember this is for side servings and you serve a one fourth piece eggplant.

4 eggplants

1 pound ham (chopped)

1 pound Shrimp deveined (chopped)

2 eggs (beaten)

2 large yellow onion (chopped)

1/2 green bell pepper (chopped)

3 stalk green onions (chopped)

4 sprigs parsley (chopped)

3 clove garlic (minced)

1 bay leaf

1/4 tsp thyme

1/2 tsp oregano

1/2 tsp paprika

1/4 tsp basil

1/2 tsp rosemary

1/4 tsp cayenne pepper

1/4 tsp black pepper

1 tsp salt

1/2 cup butter

2 cups bread crumbs (plain)

1/2 cup milk (whole)

1-2 cup water

Preheat oven to 350-375 degrees. Next bring water to boil in a Dutch Oven. Bring to a boil and add sliced eggplants (cut down the middle, lengthwise). Let boil (20 minutes). Gently remove from pot and let drain. When cool enough to handle remove the eggplant meat from its shell and put it in a bowl. Chop and set aside. Chop ham and shrimps and set them aside. Melt the butter in a large saucepan on medium heat. Add the onions and bell pepper sauteing (7-10 minutes). Add green onions, garlic, parsley, and all spices to the pan cook (4-6 minutes). Add ham to the pan cook (5 minutes). Next add shrimps continue cooking (5 minutes). Add the eggplant to the pot. Stir to keep from sticking. Next, add water milk and egg beat mixture before adding to your pan. Let cook (15-20 minutes) on low heat. Stir as you pour the mixture into the pan. Add the bread crumbs a little at a time until the right consistency is achieved. Not too wet, not too dry. Taste test and adjust with spices and salt. This is a spicy dish so please add the spiced especially cayenne pepper. Put the eggplant mixture into its shells or put the filling into a baking pan and place in the oven. Sprinkle top with bread crumbs. Bake until slightly golden brown (30-40 minutes). Remove for oven and allow the sit (5-10 minutes). Enjoy! This dish aims to please.

Yield: 12 serving

STUFFED MIRLITON

This recipe is in the Everyday section of the book.
It is because as a young child I have always eaten this dish as a side dish, but
I do know some people that it mirliton as the main course.
OMG, How this dish brings back memories of my childhood. My daddy had a mirliton vine in our back yard. At
Thanksgiving and Christmas time, daddy would have enough to give all of his neighbors and family. My brother
Charlie and I called ourselves the mirliton brigade because we took care of the vine and its trellis. Remember my daddy
was a Merchant Marine and when daddy was away working we were happy to man his ship. A mirliton vine was
of the norm in the sixth and seventh wards. Along with figs, pears, and persimmons trees were very common in all the
neighbors of New Orleans. I enjoyed this dish as a little girl and I still enjoy eating mirlitons each and every holiday.

6 mirlitons, medium size

1 pound shrimp, peeled, deveined, and diced

1/2 lb ham (chopped)

2 yellow onion (chopped)

3 stalk green onions (chopped)

1/2 bell pepper (chopped)

3 sprigs fresh parsley (minced)

2 cloves garlic (minced)

1 tsp thyme

1/2 tsp rosemary

1/4 tsp oregano

2 bay leaves

1/2 tsp cayenne

1/8 tsp black pepper

1/2 tsp salt

2 eggs, beaten

1/2 cup butter

1 cup water

2 cups bread crumbs (plain)

Preheat the oven to 350. Cut mirliton in half and place in a large saucepan. Cover with water, bring to a boil, and cook (15-25 minutes). Remove mirliton from the water and allow them to cool. When cool enough to handle, remove the pit and scoop out all the meat. Reserve the shells and set the meat aside. In a saucepan over medium heat sauté onions, bell pepper, and green onions (10 minutes) in 1/2 cup butter. Add garlic, parsley, and ham, let cook (5 minutes). Next, add mirliton, all spices, and bay leaves to the pot. Add the shrimps and cook (30 minutes). Stir occasionally to prevent sticking. Add bread crumbs and water to the pot. Taste test and adjust spices and salt. Allow simmering (15 minutes). Then stuff the mirliton halves. Next, sprinkle the remaining bread crumbs on top of your mirlitons. Bake until the crust is brown (15-20 minutes). And have it your way with one of your favorite sides.

Yield: 12 servings

STUFFED SHRIMP

Yield: 12-24 serving

Buffet table here I come! These little goodies were there center stage and on the menu, balls, weddings, anniversaries, parties, or just about any kind of celebration. Whatever the occasion the stuffed shrimp will be there. they are one of New Orlean's most popular and desired appetizers. In the home stretch with the famous oyster pattie and crab cake, they are sure tasty winners. With or without the crabmeat the stuffed shrimp is sure to please both your pallet and your appetite. Enjoy!

1/2-1 pound crabmeat (optional)

1 pound medium to large shrimp (deveined)

2 eggs lightly beaten

1 cup breadcrumb

1/2 tsp rosemary

1/8 tsp thyme

1/8 tsp oregano

1/4 tsp paprika

1/8 tsp black pepper

1/2 tsp cayenne pepper

1/4 cup butter

1/4 cup water

1 Preheat oven to 350 degrees.

2 Peel shrimp leaving tails on, devein and butterfly.

3 Lay on a greased cookie sheet to form a circle with the tail pointing up.

4 Melt the butter.

5 Mix all ingredients and taste test.

6 Add water only if needed a little at a time.

7 Place a spoonful of crabmeat mixture on top of the shrimp.

8 Place cookie sheet in the oven (15-20 minutes).

9 Remove with spatula to a serving tray to serve.

10 Also, try this recipe for stuffing mushrooms which only take (10-15 minutes) in the oven, same temp.

11 To prepare for a party, prepare trays, cover with plastic wrap, and store in the refrigerator, then just place in the oven when ready and serve. Serve warm.

STUFFED BELL PEPPER

I must truthfully say as a small child I did not eat stuffed bell peppers. I was not introduced to them until I was about fifteen. But once I tasted one I was hooked. The filling of peppers is quite similar to the filling of the mirliton. The Creole-style of using the ham and shrimp filling is the same. I love this dish. So I decided to put it in my book because so many people I know enjoy this dish. Now as an adult I do cook them as a side dish. There are many different ways of cooking peppers, but my favorite is the ham and shrimp way. Remember all dressings, and stuffings were prepared with day old french bread. Try this Creole spin and enjoy!

6 medium Green Bell Peppers

1 pound shrimp, peeled, deveined, and diced

1/2 lb ham (chopped)

2 yellow onion (chopped)

4 stalk green onions (chopped)

4 sprigs fresh parsley (minced)

3 cloves garlic (minced)

1 tsp thyme

1 tsp rosemary

1/4 tsp oregano

2 bay leaves

1/2 tsp cayenne

1/8 tsp black pepper

1/2 tsp salt

1/2 cup butter

1-2 cups water

2 cups french bread or bread crumbs (plain)

Preheat the oven to 350. Cut bell papers in half and clean. Place in a large baking pan and set aside. In a large saucepan over medium heat sauté onions and bell pepper (3-5 minutes) in butter. Add garlic, green onions, and ham, let cook (6-8 minutes). Next, add all spices, and bay leaves to the pot. Add shrimps and cook (10-15 minutes). Stir occasionally to prevent sticking. Add bread crumbs and water to the pot. Taste test and adjust spices and salt. Allow simmering (15 minutes) on low heat. Remove from heat and stuff your peppers. Next, sprinkle the remaining bread crumbs on top of your peppers. Add 1-2 cup water to the bottom of the pan to help peppers soften. Do not let the water reach filling. Put in the oven and bake (30-35 minutes) or until peppers soften and the tops are toasted. A perfect side dish for just about anything.

Yield: 12 servings

CREOLE OYSTER DRESSING

As a little girl, I would watch my mother stuff the turkey with this dressing. Back in the day, Oyster Dressing was king. I am talking about the 1950s and the early 1960s. In our neighborhood family and friends would travel from house to house enjoying all of the good holiday foods. In those days people cook with the intention of share it. At our home, Thanksgiving and Christmas visitors would come and go all day. I loved it uncles, aunts, cousins, and friends just have a beautiful and fun time. Mama's oyster dressing was the best and when she was cooking it the aroma just filled the air. All of the seasonings and spices, it was something to behold. I remember sometimes mama would fix traditional dressing too. It depended on how many people were coming over. Wonderful times together with family and friends and the aromas of delicious food filling the air was the place our home was the place to be. I need to say that in those days, all dressings were made with french bread. Then they evolved to bread crumb. Back in the date Governor Nichols way.

2 pints fresh oysters in liquid

2 yellow onions (chopped)

1/2 green bell pepper (chopped)

4 stalk green onions (chopped)

3 cloves garlic (minced)

5 sprigs fresh parsley (minced)

1/2 tsp thyme

1/4 tsp oregano

!/2 tsp rosemary

1/2 tsp cayenne pepper

1/8 tsp black pepper

1/2 tsp salt

1/2 cup butter

3 cups bread crumb or french bread

2 eggs (beaten)

2 cups water

Drain oysters and reserving liquid. Coarsely chop the oysters and set aside. Place butter in a dutch oven on medium heat. Add onions and bell peppers to the pot saute (5-7 minutes). Next add garlic, green onions, and parsley to the pot let cook on low heat (3-5 minutes). Add oysters, bay leaf, and spices stir, and let cook (5-7 minutes). Add oyster juice continue cooking. Mix one cup of water and eggs together. Stir while adding the mixture to the pot. Bring to a boil and add the second cup of water let boil (3-5 minutes). Add bread crumbs to the pot and mix well. Bring heat to low and place a cover on the pot. Let cook another (10-15 minutes). If you need more water you can add a half-cup at a time. Taste test and add spices, cayenne, and salt if needed. Taste test one more time. You can stuff your turkey with it or serve alongside it. You can put your dressing in a baking pan and run it through the oven (20-30 minutes). Set oven at 350 degrees.

Yield: 6-8 servings

TRADITIONAL CREOLE DRESSING

Oh yes, back in the days, yes my childhood days, you could not have a Thanksgiving or a Christmas without traditional stuffing in the turkey. I still can remember mama stuffing the Thanksgiving turkey. Then she would stitch it up and into the oven, it would go. There would always be leftover dressing from the turkey, which would quickly be put in a baking pan. It was scrumptious and please do not leave out the cranberries on the side. My mother made her dressing with french bread and she would put gizzards in it. That was how Creole dressing was made way back when. All of the seasoning, the spices, the chopped chicken gizzards, and the french bread all coming together in the oven; it was a treat. As time moved on it was made with bread crumbs and other meats were added. Such shrimp and ham. Orginal or the modern touch it is all good.
I guarantee!

1-2 pounds chicken gizzard (optional)

2 yellow onions (chopped)

1/2 green bell pepper (chopped)

5 stalk green onions (chopped)

4 cloves garlic (minced)

5 sprigs fresh parsley (minced)

1/2 tsp thyme

1/2 tsp oregano

1 tsp rosemary

1/2 tsp cayenne pepper

1/4 tsp black pepper

1 tsp salt

1/2 cup butter

3 cups bread crumb or french bread

2-3 cups water

Drain oysters and reserving liquid. Coarsely chop the oysters and set aside. Place butter in a dutch oven on medium heat. Add onions and bell peppers to the pot saute (5-7 minutes). Next add garlic, green onions, and parsley to the pot let cook on low heat (3-5 minutes). Add oysters, bay leaf, and spices stir, and let cook (5-7 minutes). Add oyster juice continue cooking. Mix one cup of water and eggs together. Stir while adding the mixture to the pot. Bring to a boil and add the second cup of water let boil (3-5 minutes). Add bread crumbs to the pot and mix well. Bring heat to low and place a cover on the pot. Let cook another (10-15 minutes). If you need more water you can add a half-cup at a time. Taste test and add spices, cayenne, and salt if needed. Taste test one more time. You can stuff your turkey with it or serve alongside it. You can put your dressing in a baking pan and run it through the oven (20-30 minutes). Set oven at 350 degrees

Yield: 8-10 servings

NEW ORLEANS BAKED MACARONI

I can still remember the creamy and cheesy taste of my mama's baked macaroni. Cheesy goodness at its best.. Mana would bake this dish when she prepares a roast, baked chicken, and her mouthwatering meatloaf. Back in the days, the old times used American cheese in their baked macaroni but as time went by they start using combinations of cheeses. Whatever the combination, it was always good. My favorite dish with baked macaroni was bake hen. Remember the huge hens our mothers would bake? It was so delicious and the savory gravy was to die for.

1 pound elbow macaroni

1/3 pound American, Cheddar, Colby (diced)

3 sprigs fresh parsley

4 eggs (beaten)

3 cups milk (half cream and half milk)

1/4 cup butter

1/2 tsp oregano

1/2 tsp rosemary

1/4 tsp black or white pepper

salt (pinch to taste)\

Preheat oven to 350 degrees. Put water in a pot, add salt, and bring to boil on high heat. After the water begins to boil add macaroni. Cook al dente, drain and put aside. Mix beat eggs, spices, milk, and cream together and put aside. Put macaroni in a baking pan and pour in the egg mix. Melt butter and pour into the pan. Mix while pouring into the pan and add cheeses. Mix well making sure the cheese is evenly spread in your pan. Place in oven (30-40 minutes) or until cheese is melted and the mixture is slightly firm. Remove from oven and let rest for 5 minutes before serving.

Yield: 8-10 servings

NEW ORLEANS DIRTY RICE

*This little easy to fix dish is a true hit with kids and grown-ups. This little dish makes
a great lunch or try it for breakfast just add beakfast sausage to it.*

1 pound ground beef

1/2 green bell pepper (chopped)

1 large onion (chopped)

2 stalks celery (chopped fine)

4 stalks green onions (chopped)

3 clove garlic (minced)

3 sprigs fresh parsley (chopped)

2 bay leaves

1/4 tsp sage

1/4 tsp oregano

1/2 tsp paprika

1/8 thyme

1/2 rosemary

cayenne pepper (to taste)

1/4 tsp black

1/2 tsp salt

2-3 tbsp butter (optional)

3-4 cups rice (cooked, long-grain)

1/2 cup water

Put grounded beef in a large Dutch oven on medium-high heat and let cook (5-7 minutes). If beef is very lean add butter to the pot. Add bell pepper, onions, and celery to the pot. Cook (6-8 minutes) until softened. Lower heat to medium-low. Add spices, green onions, and garlic, to the pot. Continue to cook (5 minutes) Add cooked rice, bay leaf, and continue to cook. Stirring, mix together, letting rice toast just a little. Add water to your pot. Taste test and adjust spices and salt. Turn the heat to low, cover, and simmer (15-20 minutes). Cook until the rice broth has been absorbed. Stir in the parsley and remove from heat. Dirty Rice should not be too wet or gummy. Grains should separate easily and still be moist enough to hold together on your fork. Can be served with your choice of meat or served by itself. A great thing about this simple little treat is it is even better tasting the next day.

Yield: 8-10 servings

CREOLE SMOTHERED SNAP BEANS

Smothered snap beans were definitely on the weekday household menus. Back in the days, this dish was cooked with pickled meat or ham. Either way, it served as a great satisfying meal. As a little girl, it was one of my favorites and it still is today. Mothers and grandmothers cooked every day and they loved doing it. Good cooks, good people, and good food. Those were the days. New Orleans, sixth ward creole style.

2 pounds string beans

1 pound season meat (your choice)

2-3 potatoes (diced)

1 yellow onion (chopped)

1/4 green bell pepper (chopped)

2 cloves garlic (minced)

4 sprigs parsley (chopped)

1/8 tsp oregano

1/8 tsp thyme

1/2 tsp rosemary

2 bay leaves

1/4 tsp black pepper

salt (pinch)

2 tbsp butter

1 tbsp flour (all-purpose)

1-2 cups water

Place meat in a large dutch oven. Cook and stir over medium-high heat with butter (5-6 minutes). Add onions, bell pepper to pan let cook (3-5 minutes) continue to stir. Add flour, garlic, and all spices to the pan let cook (3 minutes). Add beans, potatoes, bay leaves, and water to the pan, mix. Let the beans cook until the beans are tender. If the beans are not tender once the water has gone down. Add more water, let cook until tender. Taste test and adjust accordingly. Smother Snap Beans is served over steamed rice.

Yield: 6-8 serving

CANDIED SWEET POTATOES

Candied Sweet potatoes have always been a special treat for me. Back in the days, sweet potatoes were always cooked stovetop. This dish was used as one of the sides served with all types of roast, especially pork roast. Pork and sweet potatoes and style go hand and hand. As a little girl, I always loved my mama's way of cooking them, so buttery with a hint of vanilla. I also love my daddy's rendition of this dish. so, so good. Daddy's style called for sliced lemon and raisin together with a much heavier sauce. It was to die for. I thank God for my two worlds of cooking, Creole Style with my mama and American Traditional with my daddy. Those were the days, me, and my sweet potatoes. I must yes they can go with just about any dish and don't leave out the mustard greens. In the sixth and seventh wards, mustard greens were king.

6-8 sweet potatoes (peeled and sliced)

1 cup sugar (white/light brown)

2 tbsp ground cinnamon

1 tsp ground nutmeg

1 tsp vanilla extract (pure)

1/2 tsp salt

1 cup water

1/2 cup butter

In a small bowl, mix the sugar, cinnamon, nutmeg, and salt together. Melt butter in a large skillet over medium heat. Add sweet potatoes stir to coat. Sprinkle sugar mixture over the sweet potatoes, and stir. Pour in water into the pot. Place cover on your pot. Reduce heat to low. After (30 minutes) taste test for sweetness and spices. Stir in vanilla. Let cook (15-20 minutes) stirring occasionally. Continue cooking until potatoes are candied and tender. Serve, eat, and enjoy.

Yield: 8 serving

CREOLE BAKED POTATO

Yield: 4 servings

This little bunch of joy is great as a side dish with any meal. Truly creole the mighty baked potato, there is no doubt about it.

So simple to make yet so enjoyable.

4 large round sweet potato

2 Tbsp oil (your choice)

aluminum foil (4 pieces)

1 Prepare heat oven 350 degrees.

2 Wash 4 your potatoes.

3 Remove any blemishes or dark spots.

4 Rub the potatoes with oil.

5 Wrap potato in aluminum foil.

6 Bake (50-80 minutes) or until tender.

7 Can be served with butter.

8 You can sprinkle sweet potato with your choice of sugar, honey, cinnamon, and nutmeg.

NEW ORLEANS CREOLE DESSERTS

In this section of my book are some of the desserts of good old yesteryears.
Our mothers and grandmothers would bless their families and
friends with treats all homemade everything from scratch.

They did it with tenderness, love and care.

MAMA'S BUTTER POUND CAKE

The Mighty Poundcake is number one in my home town. It stands along with taste. It has the wonderful ability to make you think of the good old days and how mothers use to make their cakes. Just eating a slice. No matter where you are just one bite of a homemade poundcake will take you back to the good old days. I know it takes me back. Mamas and grandmas were serious about their cooking and their baking. They used nothing but the best ingredients pure vanilla, real butter, and name-brand products. My mother would only bake with brown eggs, no white eggs in my mama's cakes. The pound cake has been my favorite cake as a little girl, my favorite now, and it will be my favorite forever. Throughout our neighborhood, you could smell the aroma of the butter, and the vanilla, this was the norm. This cake would grace the tables of the houses of the creole neighborhoods. No matter how some of us added to it or took away from it, it still came out to be a delicious pound cake.

A creole poundcake is a creole poundcake, is a creole poundcake.

Now bring on the coffee with chickory!

3 1/2 cups flour (all-purpose)

3 1/2 cups sugar

3 sticks butter (soften)

4 ounces cream cheese (soften)

1 cup buttermilk

6 eggs, large

1 tbsp vanilla extract (pure)

2 teaspoon baking powder

1/2 tsp salt

1 tbsp lemon juice

Preheat oven to 350 degrees. Grease and Flour bundt pan or spray with nonstick cooking spray. In a mixer, cream butter, sugar, and cream cheese until light and fluffy. Add eggs one at a time, beat about 30 seconds between each egg. Add vanilla. In a separate bowl mix flour, baking powder, and salt. Add flour in batches alternating with buttermilk, ending with flour. Beat about 30 seconds on low between each addition. With a spoon mix mixture to incorporate any remaining flour. Then mix on medium (10-15 minutes) scraping the sides of the bowl. Pour mixture into bundt pan and bake (55-75 minutes). Check to see if the cake is ready. Remove from oven, allow to cool (7-10 minutes). Next, flip the cake out of the pan then carefully flip your cake onto a cake plate. Allow to thoroughly cool before covering. Can be served with your choice of tops. So eat up and enjoy!

Yield: 16-18 servings

7-UP POUND CAKE

The 7 Up Cake is such a wonderful tasting cake. From the lemony butter cake to the lemon/sour cheese icing dribbling down the sides, surely it is a cake that aims to please the palette, a sure winner. The 7 Up cake is one of the most popular cakes in the New Orleans area. I remember the little old ladies use to sell these cakes for a living. You had to call your order in early or you would hear the word booked! One bite and they had customers for life.

Good to the very last bite!

3 sticks butter (softened)

3 cups sugar

5 large eggs

1/2 tsp salt

2 tbsp lemon juice

1 tsp vanilla extract

3 cups flour (all-purpose)

3/4 cup 7-Up

Glaze

1-1/2 cups confectioners sugar

1 tbsp cream cheese

1 tbsp lemon juice

1/2 tsp vanilla

1/8 tsp salt (to taste)

1-2 tbsp cream

Preheat oven to 350 degrees. Grease and flour a 10 inch fluted or plain tube pan. In a large bowl, cream butter and sugar until light and fluffy. Add eggs, one at a time, beating well after each addition. Add salt to the mixture. Beat in lemon juice and vanilla, then add flour alternately with 7 Up, beating well after each addition. Transfer batter to the pan. Then bake (65-75 minutes) or until a toothpick inserted in the center comes out clean. Cool (15-20 minutes) then remove from pan. Let cool completely on a wire rack. For the glaze, mix sugar, vanilla, lemon juice, salt, and enough cream to reach the desired consistency, then drizzle over the cake.

Yield: 14-16 servings

YELLOW CAKE W/ CHOCOLATE ICING

Where's my New Orleans people? Who remembers this one. Almost every house in the city, especially the sixth and the seventh wards was noticed for the yellow (vanilla) cake with chocolate icing. Every house owned a cake plate or two or three. Every home would have a homemade cake under one, EVERY SUNDAY. This was the norm back in the day of New Orleans. My mother was into her pound cakes, but I was into this oldie but goodie. An old favorite of many. This cake went great with an ice-cold glass of milk. Coffee for the grown folks and everyone was happy.

2 cups flour (all-purpose)

1 -1/2 cup sugar

2 eggs

1 tbsp baking powder

1/2 tsp salt

1/2 cup butter (softened)

1 cup milk (whole)

2 tsp vanilla extract

For Icings

4 cup powdered Sugar

3/4 cup cocoa powder

1/4 cup butter (salted soften)

3-4 tbsp cream (evaporated) (1 tbsp at a time)

1 tsp vanilla

Preheat oven to 350 degrees. Grease and flour two 9-inch cake pans. In a large mixing bowl sift together flour, sugar, baking powder, and salt and set aside. Mix sugar and butter until fluffy (2-5 minutes). Add eggs one at a time. Add flour mix together. Next, slowly add milk to the mixture. Add vanilla and continue to mix (5-10 minutes) scraping the side of the bowl from time to time. Pour batter into prepared pans, dividing equally. Bake (30 to 35 minutes) or until a toothpick comes out clean. Cool in pans on wire racks (10 minutes). Turn out and cool thoroughly on wire racks. For Icing In a mixer, whip butter until pale and fluffy. Sift in powdered sugar and cocoa powder, followed by vanilla and heavy cream. Mix on high speed until the icing well combined. Once your cakes are thoroughly cooled you can ice your cake.

Yield: 1 9" two layered cake

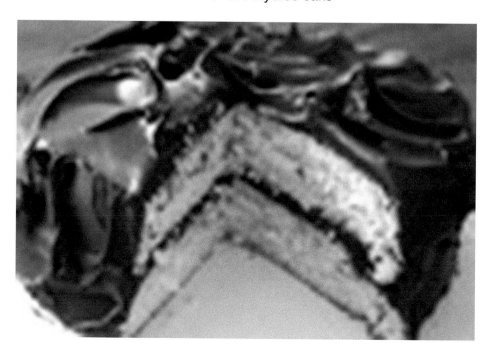

DADDY'S FRUIT CAKE

Fruit cake is a dessert, you love it or you hate it. But, if you would have tasted one of my daddy's homemade fruit cake, you would have been hooked for life. When daddy was home for the holiday, it was a joy unspeakable. Remember my father was a seaman, "Merchant Marine". So some holidays he was home and some he wasn't. I must say all of my Christmas was beautiful but daddy was home it was grand. And when he was home, he would make his delicious fruit cake. Load down with cherries, pineapples, nuts, dates, raisins, and a pinch of rum to finish it out. As a little girl, I didn't know which I liked the most the fruits or the nuts. It was all good, so very good.

1 cup dates (chopped)

1 cups raisins

1/2 cup glazed pineapples (glazed)

1 cup glazed cherries (glazed)

1/2 cup walnuts (chopped)

1/2 cup pecans (chopped)

1 tbsp fresh orange zest (grated)

2 cups flour (all-purpose)

(divided into 1/4 cup & 1 3/4 cups)

1 cup granulated sugar

2 egg (room temperature)

1 tbsp baking soda

1 cup sour cream

1/4 tsp nutmeg

1 tsp cinnamon

1/2 cup butter (room temperature)

1 tsp salt

1 tbsp vanilla

1-2 ounces Rum, Brandy (optional)

Preheat the oven to 325 degrees and prepare two standard loaf pans. Line loaf pan with greased parchment paper cut to fit the pan. Place two pieces to run the length of the pan and stand up above the rim about an inch. When the cake comes out of the oven, you can easily remove it. In a small bowl, mix together the baking soda and sour cream and set aside. Put in a bowl dates, raisins, cherries, pineapples, and nuts with 1/4 cup of the flour, toss to coat them, and Set aside. Beat together the butter and sugar until fluffy. Mix in the egg, then the sour cream/baking soda mix. Add the flour and salt and mix (5minutes). Next mix, rum/bandy, the fruit/nut mixture with creamed ingredients. Mix well to distribute the fruit and nuts evenly (3-5 minutes). Scoop the batter into the loaf pan and press down to even the surface. Place the batter-filled pan into the oven. Place a separate pan of water in the oven either on a rack underneath the fruitcake or beside it. This will help with a more even, gentle cooking. Bake for (90-105minutes), or until the straw inserted into the center **coms out** clean. Water may need to be replenished during baking. If the top of the fruitcake is getting too brown as it bakes, tent it with some foil. Remove to a rack to cool for 5 minutes. Use the edges of the parchment paper to lift the cake out of the pan. Let cool completely. Wrap tightly with plastic wrap, then aluminum to store. You can poke a few holes over the top of your cake and sprinkle a few ounces of brandy or bourbon. This will make the fruitcake moister and will help it last longer.

Yield: 16 slices

NEW ORLEANS BREAD PUDDING

The New Orleans Creole Pudding was famous as far back as the thirties. And needless to say, it is still famous today. A very much sort after dessert in the New Orleans restaurant. In the olden day, this dessert was made with day-old french bread. Loaded with butter, cream, raisins, and, vanilla, it was truly delectable. It is a have it your way sort of dish. Whether you slice it or you prefer to scoop it out of the pan, It is so good.

Ce' st si Bon!

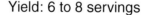

1 whole french bread (day old or older)

1 cup sugar

3-4 eggs

1 cup raisins (soaked)

1-2 tsp cinnamon

1-2 tsp vanilla

1/2 tsp salt

2-3 cups milk

3 tbsp butter (melted)

preheat oven to 350 degrees. Break bread into small pieces in a medium-size baking dish/pan. Add your soaked raisin to the pan. Add eggs, vanilla, cinnamon, and salt in a bowl and mix (3-6 minutes) then pour into pan. Pour in milk then the butter and gently mix all ingredients together. **Taste taste.** Bake (30-40 minutes) or until bread pudding sets. Serve with your favorite sauce. and enjoy!

Yield: 6 to 8 servings

NEW ORLEANS CREAM SAUCE

This sauce was the kind of sauce that was used back in the days. It was called the basic sauce for bread pudding. My mother made her sauce similar to a vanilla pudding. If you wanted it thinner add more milk. Not as rich use less butter. It is up to use. And what people would do is add the flavor they wanted to their sauce brandy, rum, and whiskey. It was whiskey and then as the years went by the brandy and rum were adopted.

2 cups milk

1/4 stick butter

1/2 cup sugar

1 tsp vanilla extract (pure)

1/2 tsp salt

1 tsp oil

2 tbsp flour (all-purpose)

Place milk, butter, salt, and sugar in a saucepan. Let come to a boil. Use the oil and flour to make a white roux. Stir in the saucepan. Let cook until thicken. Stir to keep from scorching. Remove from heat and add vanilla. Can add a few drops of yellow food coloring to give your sauce a nice creamy look. Serve over pudding.

Yield: 8 servings

NEW ORLEANS RUM SAUCE

Rum Sauce is a spinoff from the original sauce. All you are doing is adding the type of liquor you prefer. The same rules apply to the thicking and the thinning of your sauce. Also to the richness of your sauce. More butter really rich, less butter no as rich.

2 cups milk

1/2 stick butter

1/2 cup sugar

1/2 tsp salt

1 tbsp vanilla extract (pure)

Rum to taste

1 tbsp oil

2 tbsp flour (all-purpose)

Place milk, butter, salt, and sugar in a saucepan. Let come to a boil. Thicken with a light roux made of oil and flour. Taste test for flavor and sweetness. Remove from fire, add, vanilla and rum to taste. Taste test again. Serve over pudding.

Yield: 8 serving

BLACKBERRY DUMPLINGS

Fruit dumplings were very popular deserts in the fifties and sixties. Truly Creole from apple dumplings to the fig dumplings, to the raspberry dumpling, they were all good. Have you ever heard of prune dumplings? It was the Creole's favorite. I mostly remember prune dumplings, it was very good and buttery. Thank you mama for all of the good memories, good desserts, and how we could share them with all of our friends.

3- 4 cups fresh blackberries

1 cup sugar (or to taste)

2 tbsp cornstarch

2 tbsp water

2 cups water

1 tsp vanilla

2 tsp cinnamon (if using apples or peaches)

1/4 tsp salt

3 tsp butter (unsalted)

Dumplings

1 cup flour (all-purpose)

2-4 tbsp sugar

2 tsp baking powder

1/4 tsp salt

2 tbsp butter (room temperature)

1/3 cup whole milk

Put fruit and sugar into a large saucepan. Toss and let sit for 30 minutes stirring several times. Test taste can add more sugar if desired. Add the 2 cups water, lemon juice, vanilla, and salt. Stir and bring to a boil high-medium (5-10minutes). Stir in the cornstarch (mixed with 3 tbsp water). Continue to boil (3-5 minutes). Then reduce to a simmer and add the butter. Next mix the flour, sugar, baking powder, and salt together. Add butter and mix with a fork. Then add milk and mix together to form a semi dough ball. Drop spoonfuls of dumpling dough (about 10-12) on top of stewed fruit. Cover your pan and simmer (20-25 minutes) without lifting the pot cover. Uncover, remove from heat, and let rest (12-15 minutes). Spoon dumplings about into a serving bowl and spoon sauce on top.

Yield: 6-8 servings

SWEET POTATO PIE

The holiday special, the New Orleans sweet potato pie. No matter where you are, no matter where you go you are going to run into one of these mama knot me out pies. The aroma and the flavor will keep you asking for another slice. Two pieces now and take one home for later. Wonderful holidays, beautiful people, and delicious sock-it-to-me sweet potato pie.

My goodness, those were the days!

3-4 large sweet potatoes

1/2 cup sugar

1 tbsp flour (all-purpose)

2 tsp. cinnamon

1/8 tsp. nutmeg

1/4 tsp salt

3 large eggs

3 tbsp butter

1 tsp. vanilla

1/4 cup cream (evaporated)

1 9 inch pie shell (uncooked)

Heat oven to 350 degrees. Peel and cut potatoes. boil until tender on high-medium heat. Let drain and mix together all ingredients except eggs and vanilla. Mix on medium (5 minutes). Beat eggs and vanilla and pour into your mixture and mix (5-10 minutes). Then pour into the pie crust. Let bake (40 minutes) or until the center is almost set. Lower oven temperature to 325 so the crust doesn't get too brown and let bake another (10 minutes). Let your pie set until it reaches room temperature before serving. Can be served with whip cream topping. I do have to say it will turn out scrumptiously delicious every time!

Yield: 8 serving

CREOLE PUMPKIN PIE

What time is it? It's Thanksgiving time. No doubt about it. Back in the days the fifties and early sixties pumpkin pie was the traditional pie of Thanksgiving. You were not having a holiday without this buttery mouthwatering treat.

Yes, this one was a winner!

2 cup fresh pumpkin (cooked)

3 eggs

3/4 cup white sugar

2 tsp cinnamon

1/4 tsp nutmeg

1/4 tsp allspice

1/4 tsp lemon juice

1 tsp vanilla

3 tbsp butter

1/2 tsp salt

10-12 ounce milk or cream

1 9-inch pie shell (uncooked)

Preheat oven to 350 degrees. Clean, cut to remove the pumpkin from its skin, and dice into small pieces. On medium-high let boil in as little water as possible until tender. Remove from pot and let drain. Mix eggs and sugar together in a large bowl (3-5 minutes) Add salt, all spices, lemon, and vanilla to bowl, continue mixing (2-3 minutes) Next, add pumpkin and cream to the bowl. Beat together until everything is well mixed. Pour the filling into an uncooked 9-inch pie shell. Place in oven and allow to bake (55-65 minutes) or until a knife inserted in the center comes out clean. Cool your pie on a wire rack (2 hours). You will note that the pumpkin pie will come out of the oven all puffed up (from the leavening of the eggs), and will deflate as it cools. That is okay. Serve with whipped cream. And Enjoy!

Yield: 8 serves

MY DADDY'S APPLE PIE

Apple pie, who doesn't like them? From a little girl, I always enjoyed eating my daddy's apple pies, he made the best pies. The overstuffed filling with its light flaky crust was a winner for all of the holidays. All of the pies he made was twelve-inch pies. For a little girl in nursery school, his pies were humungous. I use to hold my hands up to show my classmates at school how big they were. Hats off to some of my great memories and to great apple pie.

7 to 8 apples, (peeled, cored, and sliced into 1/2-inch slices) (no tart apples)

1/2 cup sugar

1/4 cup flour (all-purpose)

2 tsp cinnamon

1/8 nutmeg

1/2 tsp vanilla

1/4 tsp salt

3 tbsp butter

2 9" pie shell

Preheat oven to 350 degrees. Mix sugar, salt, flour, cinnamon, and nutmeg into a bowl and mix together. Pour over apple and toss. Mix vanilla and water together. Place prepared apples in the unbaked shell. Cut butter in tiny, thin slices and put it on the top of the apples. Pour water mixture into the pie. Top with the second crust, and flute. Put slits in the top of the crust. Place your pie in the oven on the middle rack, do not put it on the top shelf. Bake (55-70 minutes). If the pie is browning too fast remove and a light tent or cover outside edges with foil. Then continue to bake another (25-35 minutes). Remove and place your pie on a rack to cool completely for a few hours. Serve by itself or top with ice cream.

Yield: 8 servings

MY DADDY'S PECAN PIE

My daddy's pecan pies have graced our family's holiday table for many years and they were delicious.

They were a must for Thanksgiving and the Christmas table and were enjoyed so must. All of his pies were 12" pies.

Here's to you daddy and your buttery pecan pies.

2 cups pecan halves

3 eggs

3/4 cup sugar (light brown)

1 cup corn syrup

3 tbsp butter (melted)

1 tbsp cornstarch or flour (all-purpose)

1 tbsp vanilla

1/4 tsp salt

1-9inch pie shell

Preheat oven to 350 degrees. Beat eggs in a mixing bowl. Add sugar, corn syrup, butter, and vanilla. Mix together flour and salt. Sprinkle in the mixture. Mix thoroughly on medium speed (5-10 minutes) Stir in the pecans. Pour into pie shell. Cover edges w/foil to stop premature browning (optional) Bake (50-60 minutes) or until filling is set. Let cool & enjoy!

Yield: 8 serves

MAMA'S CUSTARD PIE

Yield: 8 serving

The creamy, richness of this pie will have you coming back for more, time after time after time. My daddy uses to say, "I'll have a piece for now and I'll have a piece for later". I would just laugh because I know he meant two slices. My brother Charlie would say, "Me too" and everyone would just laugh. There were many, many happy and funny moments with my family. This is one I remembered and want to share.

Joy and happiness are what families are suppose to be about!

3 large eggs, beaten

1 (12-ounce) can of evaporated milk

3/4 cup of granulated sugar

1 tsp vanilla extract (pure)

1/4 tsp nutmeg

1/4 tsp salt

2 tbsp flour (all-purpose)

1 9inch pie shell

1 Preheat the oven to 325 degrees.

2 Punch a few holes in the pastry shell, all over with the tips of a fork.

3 This will keep it from buckling.

4 Bake (10 minutes).

5 Mix sugar, flour, nutmeg, and salt together.

6 Next, combine the eggs, milk, and vanilla into mix.

7 Mix until well blended.

8 Pour mixture into the pie shell.

9 Set the pie shell on a tray and transport it to the oven.

10 The custard filling is very liquid and runny.

11 Very carefully transfer the pie to the oven rack.

12 Bake the pie (30-40 minutes) or until a knife inserted into the center comes out clean.

13 Cool to room temperature before serving.

14 Store leftovers in the refrigerator.

MAMA'S DEEP DISH APPLE PIE

Deep Dish Apple Pie, like the ones your grandma uses to make. The ones from back in the date were made with a homemade crust. I would watch my mother from start to finish. The smell of apples, vanilla, and butter just filled the air. My daddy's pie was always 12" pies. My daddy's apple and dutch apple pies were my favorite pies as a little girl.

So, So buttery and good!

10-12 apples (peeled, cored, and sliced)

1/2 cup sugar

2 tsp cinnamon

1/4 tsp nutmeg

1/2 tsp salt

1 tsp vanilla (pure)

1/2 tsp lemon juice

2-3 tbsp flour

3 tbsp butter

1/2 cup water

1-9 1/2 x 13 inch (2 inches to 3 inches deep)

Preheat oven to 350 degrees. Put apples and lemon in a large bowl and toss. In a small bowl, combine sugars, flour, salt, cinnamon, and nutmeg. Place dough in place for your bottom crust. Put apple mixture into the baking pan or dish. Cut and slice the butter into tiny pieces and lay all over on top of apples. Mix water and vanilla pour into your pan on all four sides. Place the second crust over the top of the pie. Trim and flute edges. Cut few slits on top. Bake (40-50 minutes) or until crust is golden brown and apples are tender. Let pie cool on a wire rack. This dessert is wonderful all by itself or try it with a scoop of vanilla ice cream.

Yield: 14-16

DADDY'S RICE PUDDING

My daddy's rice pudding. I enjoyed it so much, I would eat it with my eyes close. The rich and creamy sauce with its sweet plumb raisin was surely a treat to me. I had to put this little recipe in my book because it is special to me. My daddy uses to make it just for me because he knew I loved it so much. Daddy was good and he kept his children happy.

That is what daddies are for, good cooking and a good dessert, haha!

2 cups rice (cooked)

2 large egg yoke

2 cups whole milk (or half milk and half cream)

1/3 cup sugar (to taste)

1/2 cup raisin (soaked)

1/2 tsp cinnamon

1/4 tsp nutmeg

2 tbs butter

1/2 tsp salt

1 tsp vanilla extract (pure)

Combine one cup of milk, sugar, and salt in a saucepan. Bring to a boil on high-medium. Reduce to medium heat and let cook until creamy (10 to 15 minutes). Next, beat egg yokes into the remaining one cup of cream or milk. Add to the pan. Stirring slowly to prevent sticking or scorching. Next, add the rice to the mixture and continue to stir. Add raisins, cinnamon, and nutmeg. Let cook (4-6 minutes). Continue to stir and add butter and vanilla to your saucepan. This dish can be served in three different ways. It can be served hot, at room temperature, or cold. Whatever your preference is, it is up to you. Spoon this creamy and delightful dish into a bowl and enjoy!

Yield: 6 servings

CREOLE FRIED BANANAS

Yield: 4-6 servings

Truly New Orleans, truly creole. This dish has been around decades before I was born. I can still remember it was one of my Auntie Alice and my mama's favorite. As a child, I remember waking up to the smell of cinnamon filling the air. Fried bananas were eaten with sliced or french bread. I use to sit on my Auntie Alice's lap and I would eat my bananas and her bananas too. They would drink coffee and I would drink my milk with one tablespoon of coffee with sugar. You can use this recipe for Banana Foster. Back in the days we just called it ice cream with bananas. We were children being children!

4-6 firm bananas (cut lengthwise, then halved again)

3 tbsp butter

1/3 cup sugar

1 tbsp honey

1/4 tsp cinnamon

1/2 tsp vanilla (pure)

2/3 cup flour (all-purpose)

3 tbsp water

1 Cut bananas and dust with flour and place aside. In a large frying pan put butter on low-medium heat. Add bananas to the pan. Fry just enough for them to brown. Remove from the pan and place on a plate. Continue frying until you have fried all the bananas.

2 Add sugar and cinnamon, and the remaining butter to your skillet.

3 Add two tbsp. water, reduce heat to low and let cook until sugar is dissolved (3-5 minutes).

4 Add honey and put in vanilla, two tablespoons of water.

5 Next, add your bananas.

6 Gently spoon the sauce over the bananas.

7 Serve with thin slices of french bread. This same recipe can be used over vanilla ice cream to make the famous dessert "Banana Froster".

ARDNAS CREOLE MIXES AND BLENDS

Ardnas SanJo (MARINADE & DRY RUB)

Get your SanJo working with our finger-licking Creole Marinade and Dry Rub Mix. A classic blend of herbs and spices for the lagniappe you are looking for in New Orleans Creole cooking.

Ardnas Lagnaippe (CREOLE SEASONING)

For a true taste of New Orleans flavors. A firecracker of blended flavor for your everyday cooking.

FOR ADDED INFO OR TO PLACE YOUR ORDER.

CALL OR GO ONLINE TO:

Ardnas

P. O. Box 841746

Pearland, Texas 77584

ardnas.net

1-281-809-5157

CONCLUSION

Bonjour,

I have come to the end of my childhood journey. Back in the days of New Orleans, Sixth Ward, Creole-style, everyday meals before the days of the bottle and package products. The days when everything was made from scratch and we loved it. The everyday meals and holiday dishes; their recipes, the seasonings, the spices, and how the spices and the seasonings were used in these everyday dishes. I call it the stepping stone to Creole cooking. The 101 of basic Creole cooking. Over 123 recipes for you to try and enjoy.

Bon Appetit!

In the fifties and early sixties, we could depend on our mothers and grandmothers to keep the love alive with the Sunday family dinners. This kept the Creole culture growing strong and helped to keep the Creole family together, alive, and well. We were a village and the spirit of hospitality flowed through the streets of all neighborhoods. Our New Orleans cuisine, music, and culture set us apart from the norm. You never met a stranger when coming to our city and you will always be welcome in the homes of its people. In my New Orleans' voice, I need to say everything was copacetic (koh-puh-seh-tik) back in the days. It was a term used by young adults meaning, it's fine, OK, cool, groovy.

Copacetic!

The key or bottom line to Creole cooking is in knowing the spices and seasonings of Creole cuisine and how to apply these blends to your favorite dishes. The must-have spices in Creole cooking are Oregano, Bay leaf, Thyme, Sage, Cayenne pepper (not for hotness but for spiciness), and your must-have seasonings are Yellow onions, Green onions, Garlic, and Bell peppers (green). Every other spices and seasoning falls in line according to the dish. Poultry, Soups, Some salads are where the celery comes in at, load it up. Always let your taste buds do the talking and have it your way.

C'est Bon!

For starters add your spices that are called for in the recipes a little at a time. Especially when using oregano and thyme because a little goes a long way. Get your march, get ready, get set, GO. Taste test and make it yours.

Au Revoir!

GLOSSARY

Understanding the world of Creole cooking and the day to day spices and seasoning that make it what it is...

Flavors, Armors, and Taste.

GLOSSARY

ALLSPICE

Is usually the size of a small pea and can be ground into a powder. It has a flavor much like a blend of cinnamon, nutmeg, cloves, and ginger with a mild fruity overtone. Allspice is also referred to as Jamaican pepper or peppercorns.

The pumpkin pie would not be the same without it.

BASIL

The basil leaf is known for its pungent aroma and flavor similar to mint and clove. Basil is a versatile herb well suited to tomatoes, meat dishes, and is a primary ingredient in pesto sauce. With its many uses, it is a herb that is an absolute staple in the kitchen. Whether you choose to use it in tomato dishes or in soups, you're sure to find that this is one herb you reach for again and again. Basil is widely used as a seasoning herb for a variety of other foods including soups, stews, fish, poultry, and meat.

BASTE

Basting to moisten (foods, especially meat) at intervals with a liquid (such as melted butter, fat, gravy, or pan drippings) especially during the cooking process to prevent drying and to add flavor.

BAY LEAVE

Bay leaves have the wonderful ability to bring the absolute best out of meaty flavors and warm spices in hearty dishes. Bay leaves have a taste all their own with hints of mint and thyme, aspects of coriander, clove, and even some oregano. Its sharp and savory taste is a very important part of many Creole dishes. One or two whole leaves are added to all of your smothered dishes, gumbo, beans, sauces, stews, and soups, etc... Always remember to remove before serving.

BELL PEPPER

Bell peppers and a host of pepper cousins are some of the most versatile vegetables in the kitchen. Sauté them with onions, sliced or diced in salads, soups, stews, red beans, or any kind of beans. A most in Creole cuisine.

CATFISH

This fish is one of the most popular fish in the greater New Orleans area. The next is speckled trout. It is very popular because of its mild and delicious taste. Catfish is also loved because of the limited number of bones. It can be enjoyed poached, baked, stewed, or fried. Needless to say, it is a hit in the very famous Creole dish "Couvillion" stewed fish.

CAYENNE PEPPER

Made from the dried pods of chili peppers, this fiery spice is most popular in New Orleans Creole foods. And if you don't have cayenne on your spice rack, then you are definitely missing out on a lot of culinary opportunities. It is a must-have in Creole cuisine. I use a pinch in everything I cook for spicy, not for hot.

CELERY

Celery is very similar to parsley. Celery is often used as a flavor accent for soups, chicken, and salads. The Thanksgiving stuffed turkeys would no be the same without loads of celery.

CHICORY

Chicory is the root of the endive plant. The root of the plant is roasted and ground. Chicory is added to the coffee to soften the bitter edge of the dark roasted coffee.

CHIVES

It is an herb characterized by its long green shoots that are used as a seasoning in food dishes to provide a flavor very similar to a very mild onion. Although dried chives are available, they are best as an ingredient when they are fresh.

CINNAMON

Cinnamon is commonly used to flavor foods and beverages. Although it is often used to flavor sweet dishes cinnamon can be used in savory dishes too.

FILE'

Filé powder is made from dried sassafras leaves and is a traditional thickening agent for gumbo.

GARLIC

Garlic is used widely as a flavoring in Creole cuisine. It has an intense flavor and is an essential ingredient in cooking. In the same family as onions, garlic is often cooked but can be eaten raw. Garlic is most often used as a flavoring agent but can also be eaten as a vegetable. It is used to flavor many foods, such as salad dressings, marinades, sauces, vegetables, meats, soups, and stews.

GREEN ONION

Green onions can be eaten raw in salads and as a garnish or cooked in just about every Creole dish you can name. They will add a spicy, clean, and crisp taste to your dish. You can slice them thinly to garnish and to add flavor to your dish. The Green onions and scallions are the same things, the difference is in the size of the bottom. The Green onion, scallion, and the spring family will add the punch and added taste need in any dish.

GUMBO

Nothing says New Orleans like gumbo whether File' Gumbo or Okra Gumbo. A soup-like consistency load with ham, chicken, sausages, and seafood. It has a medium roux (a blend of oil and flour cooked slowly until browned). File' gumbo is rich, heavily seasoned, and spicy. File' Gumbo gets its name from the spicy file' (powdered sassafras leaves). It used as a thickening agent in your gumbo. Your Okra Gumbo uses fresh okra and the same ingredients as the file' gumbo including the file'. Another name for okra is Fe'vi.

MINCE

Chop into very small pieces.

Mincing is a food preparation technique in which food ingredients are finely chopped into uniform pieces. Minced food is smaller pieces than diced or chopped foods.

NUTMEG

It is a hard, and aromatic nut. Nutmeg grated is used as a spice. Nutmeg is great in desserts like pies, cakes, and teas.

It is widely known for its flavor in eggnog.

OREGANO

Oregano is a member of the mint family and related to marjoram, a much milder herb. Unlike its cousin marjoram, oregano is a very bold herb with a potent flavor. It can easily overpower the flavors of other herbs and spices or the food in a dish, so it's important to cook with knowledge of the right flavor pairings to complement this herb. Because of its robust flavor, you should always avoid adding too much. A little bit of oregano goes a long way in

any dish. Oregano is a key herb in Creole cuisine.

PAPRIKA

No kitchen is complete without paprika. It's a spice rack staple – the fourth most popular spice in the world found right next to salt and pepper in many Creole cabinets. This bright red powder comes from a mild red pepper. The flavors of paprika range from sweet, to mild, to spicy hot. Paprika works wonders as a garnish, especially for food presentation and a splash of color atop soups and appetizers. And as a flavor enhancer, it performs well too. It can give off the taste of bell pepper in a dish. Paprika came along in later years in Creole cuisine. The oldie but goodie was cayenne. The true winner for spicing and garnishing.

PARSLEY

Its leaves are mostly used as a garnish. The light, fresh flavor, and its scent complement many Creole dishes and adds great appearance and food presentation to any dish.

PO-BOY

A Po-boy is the known traditional sandwich from Louisiana. From the roast beef, ham, or fried seafood, to the shrimp, fish, oysters, or crab the Po-Boy sandwich has always been a hit in New Orleans. The humble beginning of this sandwich was just the answer to a poor man's lunch. The Po-boy is made on New Orleans French bread which is known for its crisp crust and thin fluffy center.

ROSEMARY

In cooking, rosemary is used as a seasoning in a variety of dishes, such as soups, casseroles, salads, and stews. Rosemary with chicken and other poultry is great also works well with game, lamb, pork, and fish. Rosemary is a spice that came along later on in Creole cooking.

ROUX

A roux is a combination of equal parts flour and oil, the most common in Creole cooking is butter. There are three types of roux white, blonde, and brown. They all contain the same ingredients equal parts flour and oil or butter but the colors differ based on how long you allow it to cook. It is used to give body to Creole dishes and sauces.

SAGE

Sage has a pronounced herbal flavor that has an earthy and slightly peppery taste. It works well in dishes that call for a heavy spicey taste. The rich flavor of sage means a little goes a long way. Sage goes well with pork, beef, soup, and stew recipes. Sage is a must in all Creole smothered dishes.

THYME

It is a member of the mint family and a relative of oregano. Even if you cook rarely or are just beginning to build your spice collection, thyme should be one of the first herbs on your list. Think of it as a building block to a well-rounded Creole spice rack. Thyme is one of the most basic and often-used herbs in Creole cooking. It is one of the must-haves in Creole cuisine.

VANILLA

Creole-style baking is noted for the uses of vanilla (pure) in their baking goods. The next in line is almond. The wedding cakes of old were all almond-flavored.

Printed in the United States
By Bookmasters